The BIG BOOK of DESIGNS for LETTERHEADS and WEBSITES

editor
David E. Carter

art director
Suzanna M.W. Stephens

designer
Frank L. Yates

The Big Book of Designs for Letterheads and Websites
First published in 2002 by HBI,
an imprint of HarperCollins Publishers
10 East 53rd Street
New York, NY 10022-5299

Distributed in the U.S. and Canada by
Watson-Guptill Publications
770 Broadway
New York, NY 10003-9595
Tel: (800) 451-1741
            (732) 363-4511 in NJ, AK, HI
Fax: (732) 363-0338

ISBN: 0-8230-0488-0

Distributed throughout the rest of the world by
HarperCollins International
10 East 53rd Street
New York, NY 10022-5299
Fax: (212) 207-7654

ISBN: 0-06-620941-2

First published in Germany by Nippan
Nippon Shuppan Hanbai
Deutschland GmbH
Krefelder Strasse 85
D-40549 Dusseldorf
Tel: (0211) 5048089
Fax: (0211) 5049326
nippan@t-online.de

ISBN: 3-935814-09-7

Printed in Hong Kong by Everbest Printing Company through Four Colour
Imports, Louisville, Kentucky.

The internet has brought massive changes to the business world. Even though dot-com retailers have taken a beating in the stock market from time to time, more and more people are buying merchandise online. Virtually every business has its own website.

A less subtle, internet-driven change has come to the world of letterheads. When was the last time you sent a business letter? How many do you send a month now?

Has e-mail replaced your standard first-class mail letter? The answer is most likely "yes".

While e-mail has replaced business mail, ironically, personal presentations have become more important. So, while the press runs are now smaller for letterheads and envelopes, the quantity of business cards being printed has increased. And, the use of presentation folders has become much more common.

This started out to be a big book on letterheads. The more we (my publisher and I) talked about the concept, the more we realized that the function of the letterhead set is changing, and some of that function is being replaced by the fax, by e-mail, by presentation folders, and by websites.

As designers, we must constantly reinvent ourselves; we must change to keep ahead of the curve. This book was designed to be a comprehensive reference on how designers have created consistent identities using both paper and pixels.

In design, the only constant is change. May we all profit from change, rather than being victims of it.

Client
Imageware
Design Firm
McDill Design
Milwaukee, Wisconsin
Designer
Brad Bedessem

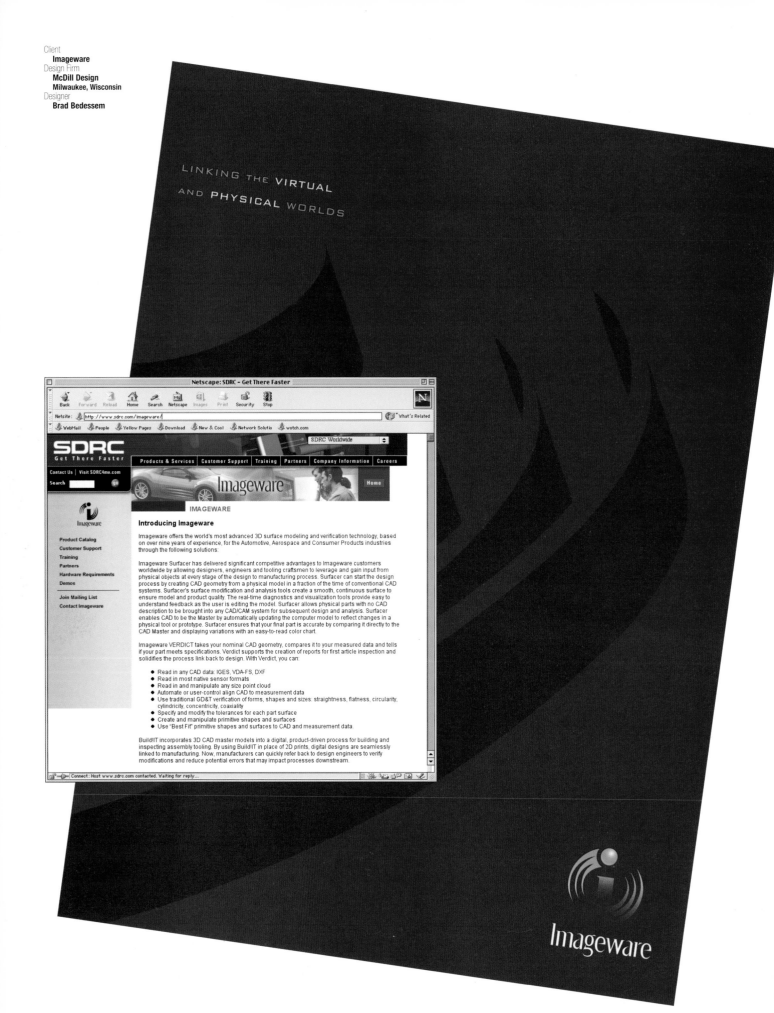

LINKING THE VIRTUAL AND PHYSICAL WORLDS

Imageware

LINKING THE VIRTUAL AND PHYSICAL WORLDS

Breakthrough Solutions

for the Challenges in the

Aerospace Industry:

Reduce time to market

Lower design time

Preserve product quality

121 West Washington
Ann Arbor Michigan 48104
Phone 313 994 7300
Fax 313 994 7303
E-Mail sales@iware.com

Veneklasen Associates
Consultants in Acoustics

1711 Sixteenth Street
Santa Monica, CA 90404

Tel: 310.450.1733
Fax: 310.396.3424

jortega@veneklasen-assoc.com

Jose C. Ortega
Managing Principal

Veneklasen Associates
Consultants in Acoustics

TRANSMITTAL

To:

We are sending you:

☐ Attached

☐ Prints   ☐ Plans

☐ Sketches   ☐ Shop drawings

☐ Copy of letter

☐ Specifications

☐ Samples

☐ _____

Copies	Date	No.	Description

Veneklasen Associates
Consultants in Acoustics

1711 Sixteenth Street
Santa Monica, CA 90404

☐ No exceptions taken

☐ Make corrections noted

Signed:

Veneklasen Associates
Consultants in Acoustics

1711 Sixteenth Street
Santa Monica, CA 90404

Tel: 310.450.1733
Fax: 310.396.3424

Veneklasen Associates
Consultants in Acoustics

Date:

Project:

VA Project No:

☐ Under separate cover via _____

☐ Revise & resubmit

☐ _____

Client
Veneklasen Associates
Design Firm
Kristin Odermatt Design
Santa Monica, California
Designers
Kristin Odermatt, Deanna McClure

Veneklasen Associates
Consultants in Acoustics
1711 Sixteenth Street
Santa Monica, CA 90404

1711 Sixteenth Street
Santa Monica, CA 90404

Tel: 310.450.1733
Fax: 310.396.3424

Client
Seattle Public Library
Design Firm
Girvin, Inc.
Seattle, Washington
Designers
Tim Girvin, Rob Berreth

SEATTLE PUBLIC LIBRARY FOUNDATION
1000 4TH AVE. SEATTLE, WA. 98104

SEATTLE PUBLIC LIBRARY FOUNDATION
1000 4TH AVE. SEATTLE, WA. 98104

WITH POSSIBILITY.
TLE'S LIBRARIES

PLACES **ALIVE** WITH POSSIBILITY.
IMAGINE SEATTLE'S LIBRARIES

SEATTLE PUBLIC LIBRARY FOUNDATION

SEATTLE PUBLIC LIBRARY FOUNDATION

TERI MOORE
DIRECTOR, CORPORATE & FOUNDATION RELATIONS
Teri.Moore@spl.org

1000 4TH AVE.
SEATTLE, WA. 98104
T.206.615.1620
F.206.386.4132

PLACES **ALIVE** WITH POSSIBILITY.
IMAGINE SEATTLE'S LIBRARIES

Deborah I. Forsten

Director of Public Relations
and Communications

10 South Broadway

Suite Number 1000

St. Louis, Missouri 63102

314 / 992-0685

Fax / 421-0394

h Broadway   Suite Number 1000   St. Louis, Missouri 63102   314 / 992-0687   Fax / 421-0394

Client
St. Louis Sports
Commission
Design Firm
Phoenix Creative
St. Louis, Missouri
Designer
Ed Mantels-Seeker

Client
30sixty design
Design Firm
30sixty design inc.
Los Angeles, California
Art Director, Designer
Pär Larsson

www.30sixtydesign.com

2801 cahuenga blvd. west

los angeles, ca 90068

voice 323 850 5311

fax 323 850 6638

www.30sixtydesign.com   2801 cahuenga blvd. west   los angeles, ca 90068   voice 323 850 5311   fax 323 850 6638

www.30sixtydesign.com   2801 cahuenga blvd. west   los angeles, ca 90068   voice 323 850 5311   fax 323 850 6638

11

B.D. Howes IV, DDS
Founder and Chairman

39331 Fawnridge Circle
Leona Valley, CA 93551

tel: (661) 266-2957
fax: (661) 266-4753
bdhowes@izyx.com

39331 Fawnridge Circle   tel: (661) 266-2957   web: izyx.com
Leona Valley, CA 93551   fax: (661) 266-4753

Client
  izyx
Design Firm
  Treehouse Design/
  Evenson Design Group
  Culver City, California
Designer
  Tricia Rauen

39331 Fawnridge Circle
Leona Valley, CA 93551

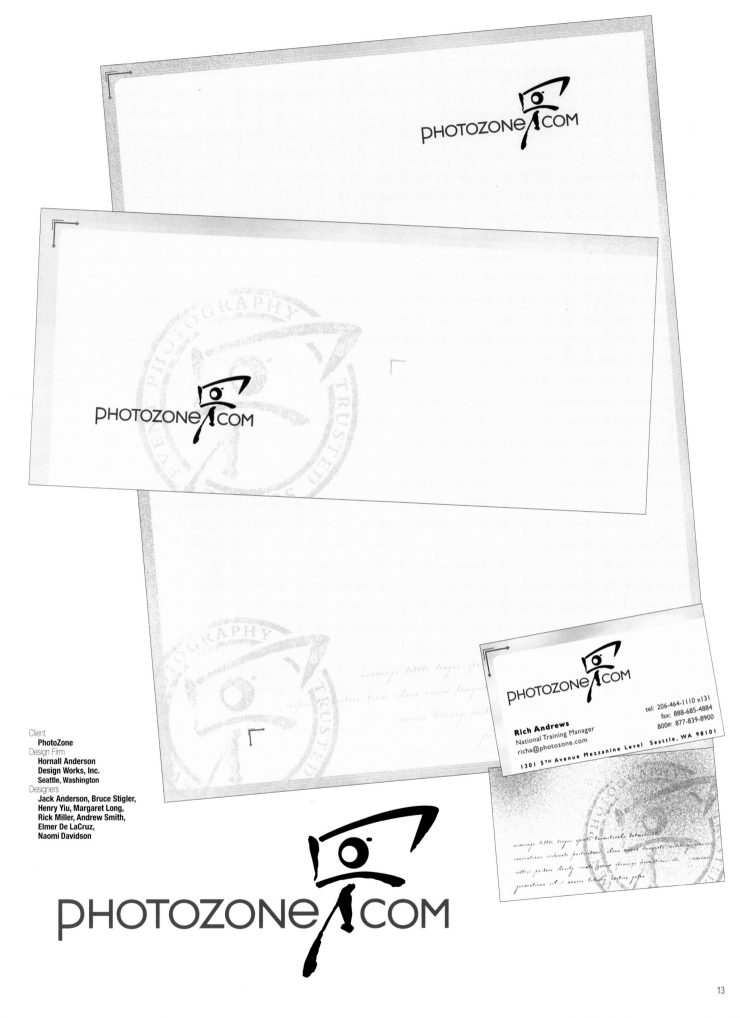

Client
PhotoZone
Design Firm
**Hornall Anderson
Design Works, Inc.
Seattle, Washington**
Designers
**Jack Anderson, Bruce Stigler,
Henry Yiu, Margaret Long,
Rick Miller, Andrew Smith,
Elmer De LaCruz,
Naomi Davidson**

Rich Andrews
National Training Manager
richa@photozone.com

tel: 206-464-1110 x131
fax: 888-685-4884
800#: 877-839-8900

1301 5TH Avenue Mezzanine Level Seattle, WA 98101

Jensen Design Associates, Inc.

320 East
Bixby Road
Long Beach
California
90807

New Media • Corporate & Brand Identity • Packaging & POP • Collateral & Advertising

Jensen Design Associates, Inc.

320 East
Bixby Road
Long Beach
California
90807

Voice
562.490.3706
Fax
562.424.5303
Modem
562.989.2917
Web
www.jensendesign.com

Client
**Jensen Design
Associates, Inc.**
Design Firm
**Jensen Design
Associates, Inc.
Long Beach, California**
Designer
David Jensen

Jensen Design Associates, Inc.

**Ann
Taono**
Office
Manager

320 East
Bixby Road
Long Beach
California
90807

Tel   562.490.3706
Fax   562.424.5303
Email a_taono@jensendesign.com
Web   www.jensendesign.com

New Media | Corporate Identity | Brand Strategy | Packaging | Point of Purchase | Collateral

New Media • Corporate & Brand Identity • Packaging & POP • Collateral & Advertising

THE ARGENT HOTEL
SAN FRANCISCO

50 Third Street
San Francisco
California
94103-3198
415.974.6400

50 Third Street
San Francisco, California
94103-3198

Client
The Argent Hotel/
San Francisco
Design Firm
Fleishman-Hillard
Design, St. Louis
St. Louis, Missouri
Designers
Paul Scherfling
Kevin Kampwerth

THE ARGENT HOTEL
SAN FRANCISCO

50 Third Street

San Francisco

California

94103-3198

415.974.6400

Client
Pepper Hamilton LLP
Design Firm
Greenfield/Belser Ltd.
Washington, D.C.
Designers
Burkey Belser, Kathy Stimson

Pepper Hamilton LLP
Attorneys at Law

Hamilton Square
600 Fourteenth Street, N.W.
Washington, DC 20005-2004
202.220.1200
Fax 202.220.1665

Pepper Hamilton LLP
Attorneys at Law

Hamilton Square
600 Fourteenth Street, N.W.
Washington, DC 20005-2004

Pepper Hamilton LLP
Attorneys at Law

Philadelphia, Pennsylvania   Detroit, Michigan   New York, New York   Pittsbu

Berwyn, Pennsylvania   Cherr

Pepper Hamilton LLP
Attorneys at Law

3000 Two Logan Square
Eighteenth and Arch Streets
Philadelphia, PA 19103-2799
215.981.4000
Fax 215.981.4750

Philadelphia, PA   Washington, DC   Detroit, MI   New York, NY   Pittsburgh, PA
Wilmington, DE   Harrisburg, PA   Berwyn, PA   Cherry Hill, NJ
www.pepperlaw.com

Philadelphia, PA   Washington, DC   Detro
Wilmington, DE   Harrisburg, PA
www.pepper

Pepper Hamilton LLP
Attorneys at Law

Mary Beth Pratt
Chief Marketing Officer

3000 Two Logan Square
Eighteenth and Arch Streets
Philadelphia, PA 19103-2799
215.981.4000
Fax 215.981.4750

215.981.4665
prattmb@pepperlaw.com

19

RANDI WOLF • GRAPHIC DESIGNER

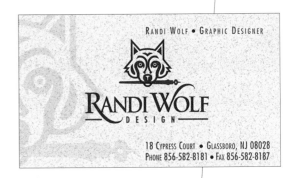

RANDI WOLF • GRAPHIC DESIGNER

18 CYPRESS COURT • GLASSBORO, NJ 08028
PHONE 856-582-8181 • FAX 856-582-8187

18 CYPRESS COURT • GLASSBORO, NJ 08028

18 CYPRESS COURT • GLASSBORO, NJ 08028
PHONE 609-582-8181 • FAX 609-582-8187

Client
   Randi Wolf Design
Design Firm
   Randi Wolf Design
   Glassboro, New Jersey
Designer
   Randi Wolf

20

Client
Technology Advancement Group
Design Firm
Pollman Marketing Arts, Inc.
Boulder, Colorado
Designer
Jennifer Pollman

Smart Business Solutions

Jacqueline A. Cotshott
Technology Consultant

Technology Advancement Group, LLP
Smart Business Solutions

P.O. Box 366 • Allenspark, CO 80510
P.O. Box 1839 • Boulder, CO 80306
Voice: 303.747.0483 • Fax: 303.747.0491
E-mail: jacqueline@TAgroup.com

Technology Advancement Group, LLP
Smart Business Solutions

P.O. Box 366 • Allenspark, CO 80510
P.O. Box 1839 • Boulder, CO 80306
Voice: 303.747.0483 • Fax: 303.747.0491
E-mail: solutions@TAgroup.com • www.TAgroup.com

Sacramento
Chico
Concord
Redding
Berkeley
Stockton
Redwood City
Reno
Monterey
Santa Rosa
San Luis Obispo
San Rafael
Bakersfield
San Jose
Fresno
San Francisco

GIANTS

1-877-TO-PITCH

Client
San Francisco Giants/Pacific Bell
Design Firm
Fleishman-Hillard Design, St. Louis
St.Louis, Missouri
Designers
Buck Smith, Kevin Kampwerth

FEBRUARY-APRIL
2000

Client
Timbuktuu Coffee Bar
Design Firm
Sayles Graphic Design
Des Moines, Iowa
Art Director, Designer, Illustrator
John Sayles

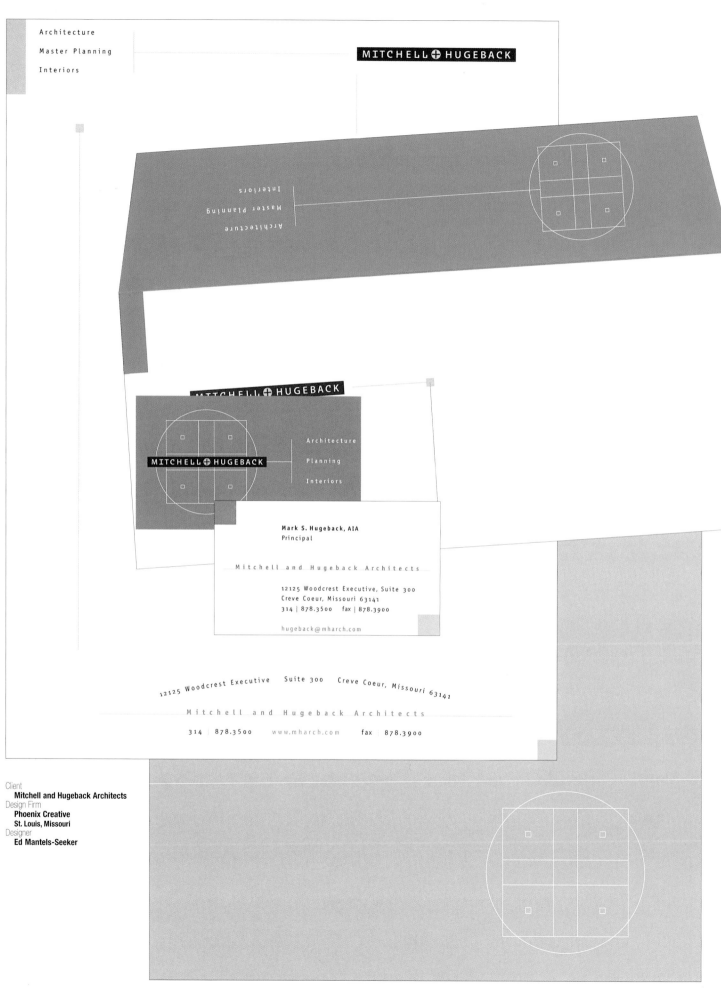

Architecture

Master Planning

Interiors

MITCHELL ✚ HUGEBACK

Interiors
Master Planning
Architecture

MITCHELL ✚ HUGEBACK

MITCHELL ✚ HUGEBACK

Architecture

Planning

Interiors

Mark S. Hugeback, AIA
Principal

Mitchell and Hugeback Architects

12125 Woodcrest Executive, Suite 300
Creve Coeur, Missouri 63141
314 | 878.3500   fax | 878.3900

hugeback@mharch.com

12125 Woodcrest Executive   Suite 300   Creve Coeur, Missouri 63141

Mitchell and Hugeback Architects

314 | 878.3500   www.mharch.com   fax | 878.3900

Client
Mitchell and Hugeback Architects
Design Firm
Phoenix Creative
St. Louis, Missouri
Designer
Ed Mantels-Seeker

290 Woodcliff Drive
Fairport, New York 14450
Phone: 716-248-9600
1-800-248-9602
Fax: 716-248-9199
www.xelus.com

Lisa Schaertl
Marketing Operations Manager

direct: 716-419-3317
fax: 716-419-3192
e-mail: lisa_schaertl@xelus.com

Client
Xelus
Design Firm
McElveney & Palozzi Design Group, Inc.
Rochester, New York
Creative Director
William McElveney
Art Directors
Matt Nowicki, Lisa Williamson
Designer
Lisa Williamson
Website Designers
Xelus

Client
Whitney Stinger, Inc.
Design Firm
Whitney Stinger, Inc.
St. Louis, Missouri
Designers
Mike Whitney, Karl Stinger

SAYLES GRAPHIC DESIGN
3701 BEAVER AVENUE
DES MOINES, IOWA 50310

(515) 279-2922 FAX: 279-0212

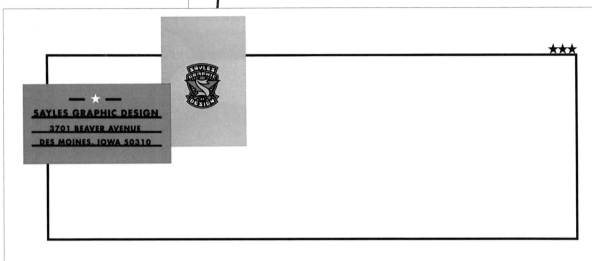

Client
Sayles Graphic Design
Design Firm
Sayles Graphic Design
Des Moines, Iowa
Art Director, Designer, Illustrator
John Sayles

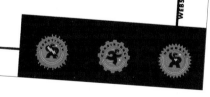

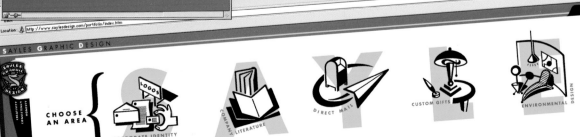

ABACUS

Client
Abacus
Design Firm
David Carter Design Assoc.
Dallas, Texas
Designers
Emily Cain

ABACUS

4557 46TH AVENUE N.E.
SEATTLE, WASHINGTON 98105

VOICE: 206.527.8286
FAX: 206.524.6641

CARY PILLO LASSEN
ILLUSTRATOR

4557 46TH AVENUE N.E.
SEATTLE, WASHINGTON 98105

VOICE: 206.527.8286
FAX: 206.524.6641

CARY PILLO LASSEN
ILLUSTRATOR

4557 46TH AVENUE N.E.
SEATTLE, WASHINGTON 98105

VOICE: 206.527.8286
FAX: 206.524.6641

CARY PILLO LASSEN
ILLUSTRATOR

CARY PILLO LASSEN
ILLUSTRATOR

4557 46TH AVENUE N.E.
SEATTLE, WASHINGTON 98105

VOICE: 206.527.8286
FAX: 206.524.6641

ESTIMATE

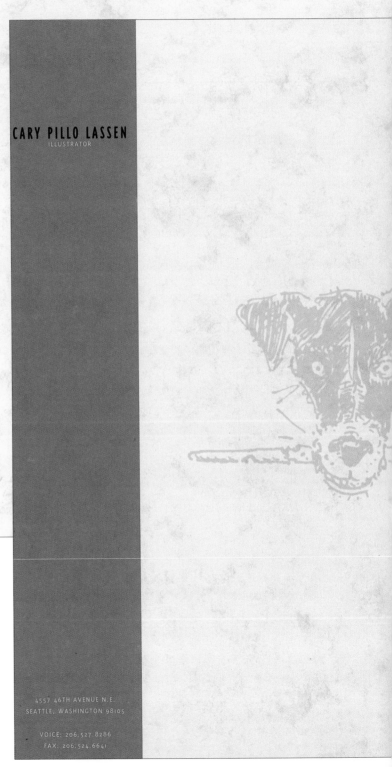

CARY PILLO LASSEN
ILLUSTRATOR

4557 46TH AVENUE N.E.
SEATTLE, WASHINGTON 98105

VOICE: 206.527.8286
FAX: 206.524.6641

Client
  Cary Pillo Lassen
Design Firm
  Belyea
  Seattle, Washington
Art Director
  Patricia Belyea
Designer
  Tim Ruszel

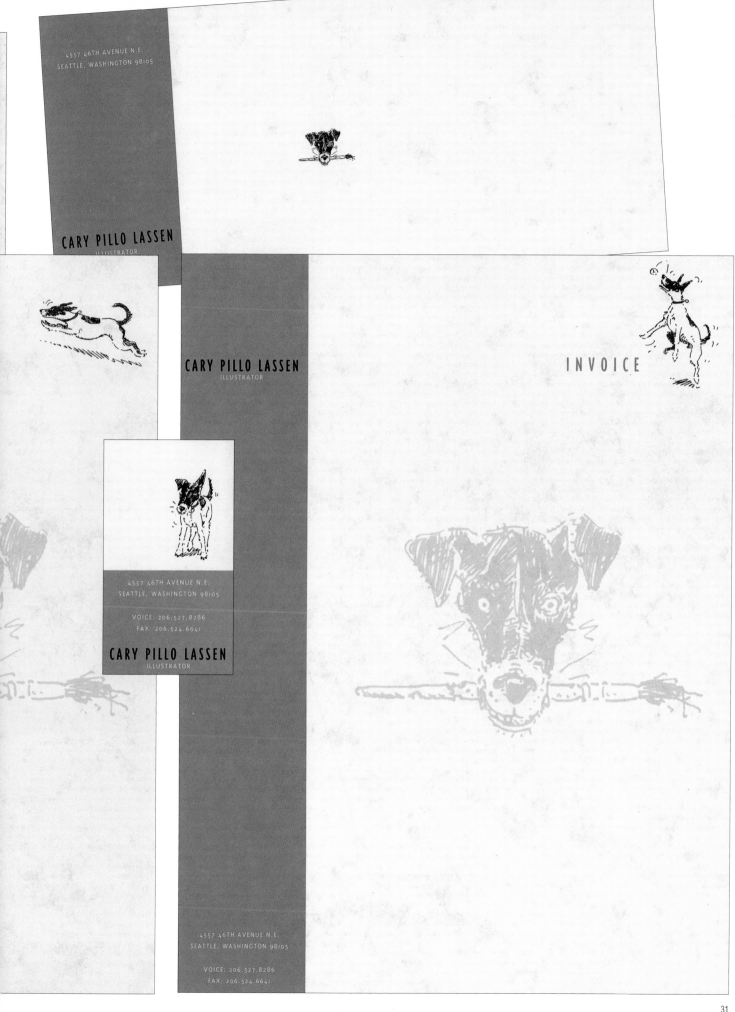

4557 46TH AVENUE N.E.
SEATTLE, WASHINGTON 98105

CARY PILLO LASSEN
ILLUSTRATOR

CARY PILLO LASSEN
ILLUSTRATOR

INVOICE

4557 46TH AVENUE N.E.
SEATTLE, WASHINGTON 98105

VOICE: 206.527.8286
FAX: 206.524.6641

CARY PILLO LASSEN
ILLUSTRATOR

4557 46TH AVENUE N.E.
SEATTLE, WASHINGTON 98105

VOICE: 206.527.8286
FAX: 206.524.6641

Beach House

Beach House

BEACH HOUSE INN & CONFERENCE CENTER
4100 NORTH CABRILLO HIGHWAY P.O. BOX 129
HALF MOON BAY, CALIFORNIA 94019-0129

Beach House

BEACH HOUSE
INN & CONFERENCE CENTER

4100 NORTH CABRILLO HIGHWAY
HALF MOON BAY, CALIFORNIA 94019

TEL 415.712.0220
FAX 415.712.0693
800.315.9366

VIEW@BEACH-HOUSE.COM

Client
Beach House
Design Firm
AERIAL
San Francisco, California
Designer
Tracy Moon

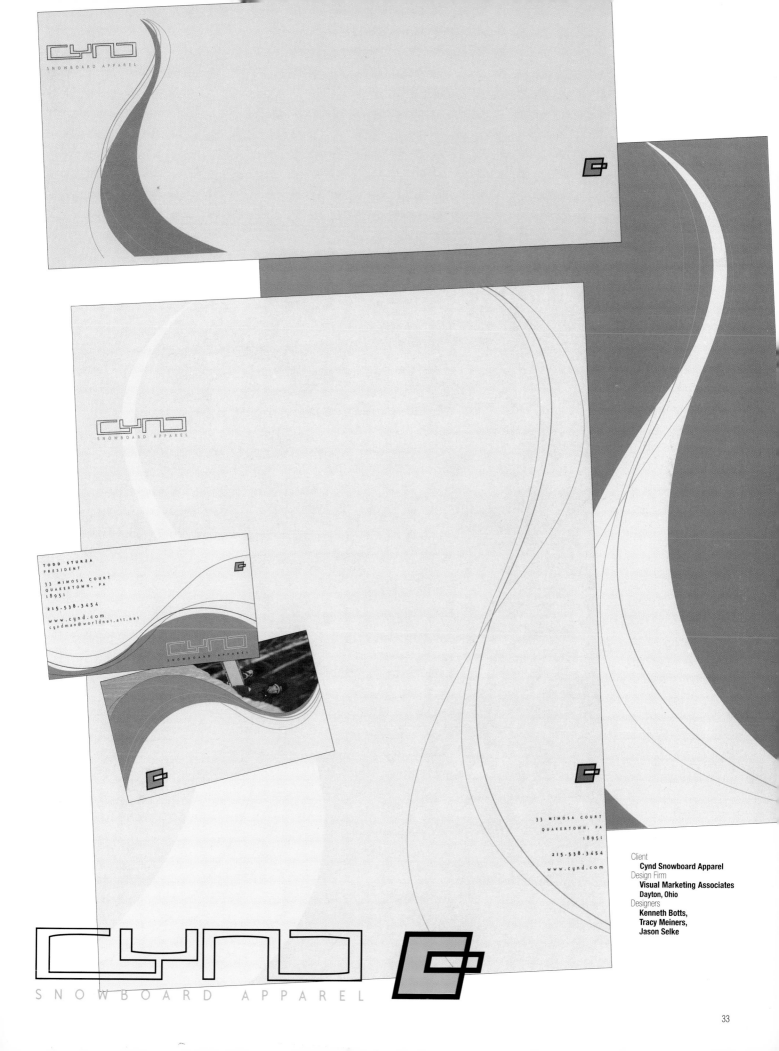

TODD STURZA
PRESIDENT

33 MIMOSA COURT
QUAKERTOWN, PA
18951

215-538-3454
www.cynd.com
cyndman@worldnet.att.net

33 MIMOSA COURT
QUAKERTOWN, PA
18951

215-538-3454
www.cynd.com

Client
Cynd Snowboard Apparel
Design Firm
Visual Marketing Associates
Dayton, Ohio
Designers
Kenneth Botts,
Tracy Meiners,
Jason Selke

the Coves
OF BRIGHTON BAY

10901 BRIGHTON BAY BLVD
ST. PETERSBURG, FLORIDA

10901 BRIGHTON BAY BLVD., N.E. ✳ ST. PETERSBURG, FLORIDA 33716
TEL 727-217-4000 ✳ FAX 727-217-4100

Client
Centex Multi-Family Co.
Design Firm
VWA Group
Dallas, Texas
Designer
Bret Sano

10901 Brighton Bay Blvd., N.E.

St. Petersburg, Florida 33716

the Coves
OF BRIGHTON BAY

Stephanie Gifford
Assistant Property Manager

the Coves
OF BRIGHTON BAY

10901 Brighton Bay Blvd., N.E. ❖ St. Petersburg, Florida 33716
TEL 727-217-4000 ❖ FAX 727-217-4100

Vista.com

Vista.com

Client
Vista.com
Design Firm
Girvin, Inc.
Seattle, Washington
Designers
Kevin Henderson,
Brent McCoy

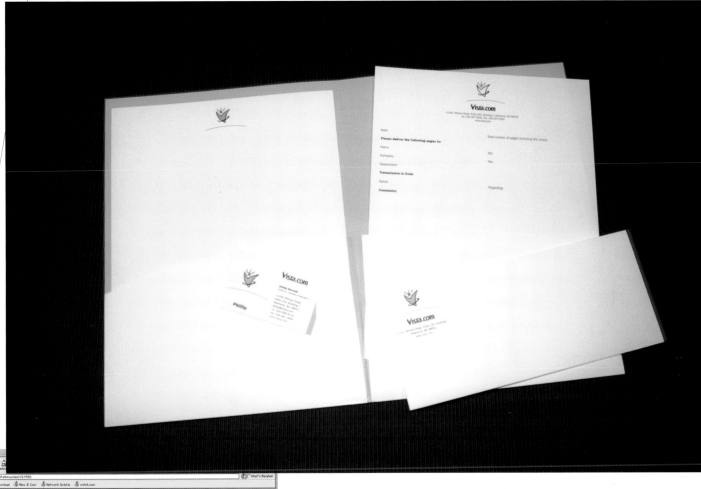

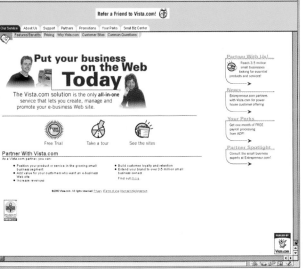

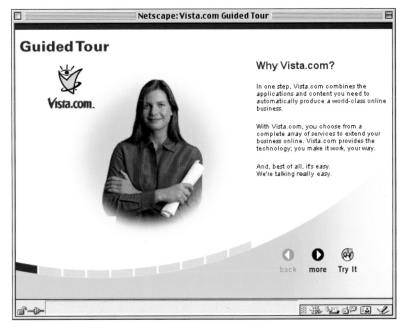

Guided Tour

Why Vista.com?

In one step, Vista.com combines the applications and content you need to automatically produce a world-class online business.

With Vista.com, you choose from a complete array of services to extend your business online. Vista.com provides the technology; you make it work, your way.

And, best of all, it's easy.
We're talking really easy.

Client
1999 Iowa State Fair
"Knock Yourself Out"
Design Firm
Sayles Graphic Design
Des Moines, Iowa
Art Director, Designer, Illustrator
John Sayles

Client
Simply Cruises
Design Firm
Phoenix Creative
St. Louis, Missouri
Designer
Ed Mantels-Seeker

SIMPLY CRUISES
3814 Hampton
Saint Louis
Missouri 63109
Facsimile:
314 832-8182
Toll Free:
1 888 367-9398

— JIM THRELKELD —
Cruise Consultant
314 832-8880

SIMPLY CRUISES

Call Us At Any Time
314 832-8880

14 Hampton Avenue
int Louis
issouri 63109-1409

lephone:
4 832-8880

csimile:
4 832-8182

ll Free:
888 367-9398

3814 Hampton Avenue
Saint Louis, MO 63109

SIMPLY CRUISES

Always At Your Service

Client
Cutler Travel Marketing
Design Firm
Sayles Graphic Design
Des Moines, Iowa
Art Director, Designer, Illustrator
John Sayles

Copper.Sky

Client
Copper Sky Grill
Design Firm
**Hornall Anderson
Design Works, Inc.
Seattle, Washington**
Designers
**John Hornall,
Larry Anderson,
Bruce Stigler,
Mary Chin Hutchison**

550 NE NORTHGATE WAY
SEATTLE, WA 98125

550 NE NORTHGATE WAY
SEATTLE, WA 98125
PH.: 206.363.9911
FAX: 206.363.9828

artworks ad agency

300 West Central Texas Expressway   Killeen, Texas 76541

Client
  Artworks Advertising
Design Firm
  Artworks Advertising
  Killeen, Texas
Designers
  Keith Dotson, Clifford Fudge

1980 2000
YEARS

artworks

Fax

To: _____ From: _____ Date: _____

Company: _____

_er: _____ # Pages: _____

artworks ad agency

BRENDA B. WHEELER
Senior Account Manager
brenda@artworks-ad.com

300 West Central Texas Expressway
Killeen, Texas 76541
• 254 • 634-5110
• 254 • 634-2440 fax
www.artworks-ad.com

www.artworks-ad.com

• 254 • 634-2440 fax

• 254 • 634-5110

76541

300 West Central Texas Expressway
Killeen, Texas 76541
• 254 • 634-5110
• 254 • 634-2440 fax
www.artworks-ad.com

1980
twenty years of
advertising excellence
2000
Y E A R S

artworks ad agency
300 West Central Texas Expressway   Killeen, Texas 76541

agenc

impli

impli

Doug Rowan
Chief Executive Officer
10439 N.E. 52nd Street
Kirkland, WA 98033
t: 425.889.1275
f: 425.889.0322
e: doug.rowan@accessone.com
w: www.impli.com

534 Fourth Street
San Francisco, CA
94107-1621
t: 415.972.1000
f: 415.972.1099
www.impli.com

Client
Impli
Design Firm
**Hornall Anderson Design Works, Inc.
Seattle, Washington**
Designers
**Jack Anderson, Sonja Max,
Kathy Saito, Alan Copeland**

Costanoa

P.O. Box 842
2001 Costanoa Road at Hwy 1
Pescadero, CA 94060

Costanoa

Sandy Chun
Front Office Manager
direct 650.879.1100

P.O. Box 842
2001 Costanoa Road at Hwy 1
Pescadero, CA 94060
reservations 800.738.7477
fax 650.879.2275

www.costanoa.com

Costanoa
Coastal Lodge & Camp

Client
  **Joie de Vivre
  Hospitality**
Design Firm
  **Hunt Weber Clark
  Assoc., Inc.
  San Francisco,
  California**
Designers
  **Nancy Hunt–Weber,
  Christine Chung**

P.O. Box 842   2001 Costanoa Road at Hwy 1, Pescadero, CA 94060   650.879.1100   fax 650.879.2275   reservations 800.738.7477
www.costanoa.com

A Catholic, Not-for-Profit Skilled Nursing Care Facility   Sponsored by the Sisters of Charity of the Incarnate Word

Saint Theresa's at South Gate

5943 Telegraph Road   *Skilled Nursing Care*   St. Louis, MO 63129

DeDee Mathews
Administrator
Saint Theresa's at South Gate

5943 Telegraph Road
St. Louis, Missouri 63129
846-2000 Telephone
846-4661 Facsimile
Area Code 314

Saint Theresa's at South Gate

5943 Telegraph Road   *Skilled Nursing Care*   St. Louis, MO 63129
846-2000 Telephone   Area Code 314   846-4661 Facsimile

A Service of Incarnate Word Hospital

Client
**Saint Theresa's at
South Gate**
Design Firm
**Kiku Obata and
Company**
St. Louis, Missouri
Designer
Ed Mantels–Seeker

COOLFISH
GRILLE • WINE BAR

Thomas G. Schaudel
Owner / Chef

COOLFISH
GRILLE • WINE BAR

6800 Jericho Turnpike
Syosset, NY 11791
T 516-921-3250 F 516-921-1004

It's hot

W W W . T O M S C H A U D E L . C O M

COOLFISH
GRILLE • WINE BAR

6800 Jericho Turnpike
Syosset, NY 11791
T 516-921-3250 F 516-921-1004

Client
**CoolFish Grille and
Wine Bar**
Design Firm
Adkins/Balchunas
Providence, Rhode Island
Designers
**Michelle Phaneuf,
Jerry Balchunas**

COOLFISH
GRILLE • WINE BAR
It's hot

ECLECTIC, INSPIRED CUISINE
STEAKS • POULTRY • SEAFOOD
AWARD WINNING WINE LIST
MARTINIS • CRAFT BEERS
LUNCH + DINNER + CATERING

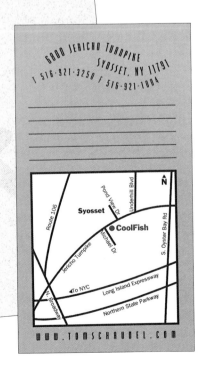

6800 Jericho Turnpike
Syosset, NY 11791
T 516-921-3250 F 516-921-1004

Route 106 — Syosset — Pond View Dr — Underhill Blvd
● CoolFish
Michael Dr
Jericho Turnpike
← To NYC
Broadway
Long Island Expressway
S. Oyster Bay Rd
Northern State Parkway

W W W . T O M S C H A U D E L . C O M

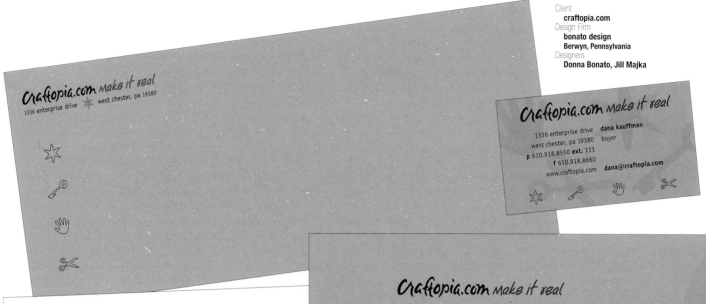

Client
craftopia.com
Design Firm
bonato design
Berwyn, Pennsylvania
Designers
Donna Bonato, Jill Majka

Craftopia.com *make it real*

1336 enterprise drive **dana kauffman**
west chester, pa 19380 buyer
p 610.918.8550 **ext. 111**
f 610.918.8660

www.craftopia.com dana@craftopia.com

NEWS

1336 enterprise drive   west chester, pa 19380   **p** 610.918.8550   **f** 610.918.8660   www.craftopia.com

1336 enterprise drive   west chester, pa 19380   **p** 610.918.8550   **f** 610.918.8660   www.craftopia.c

Craftopia.com

Lantana

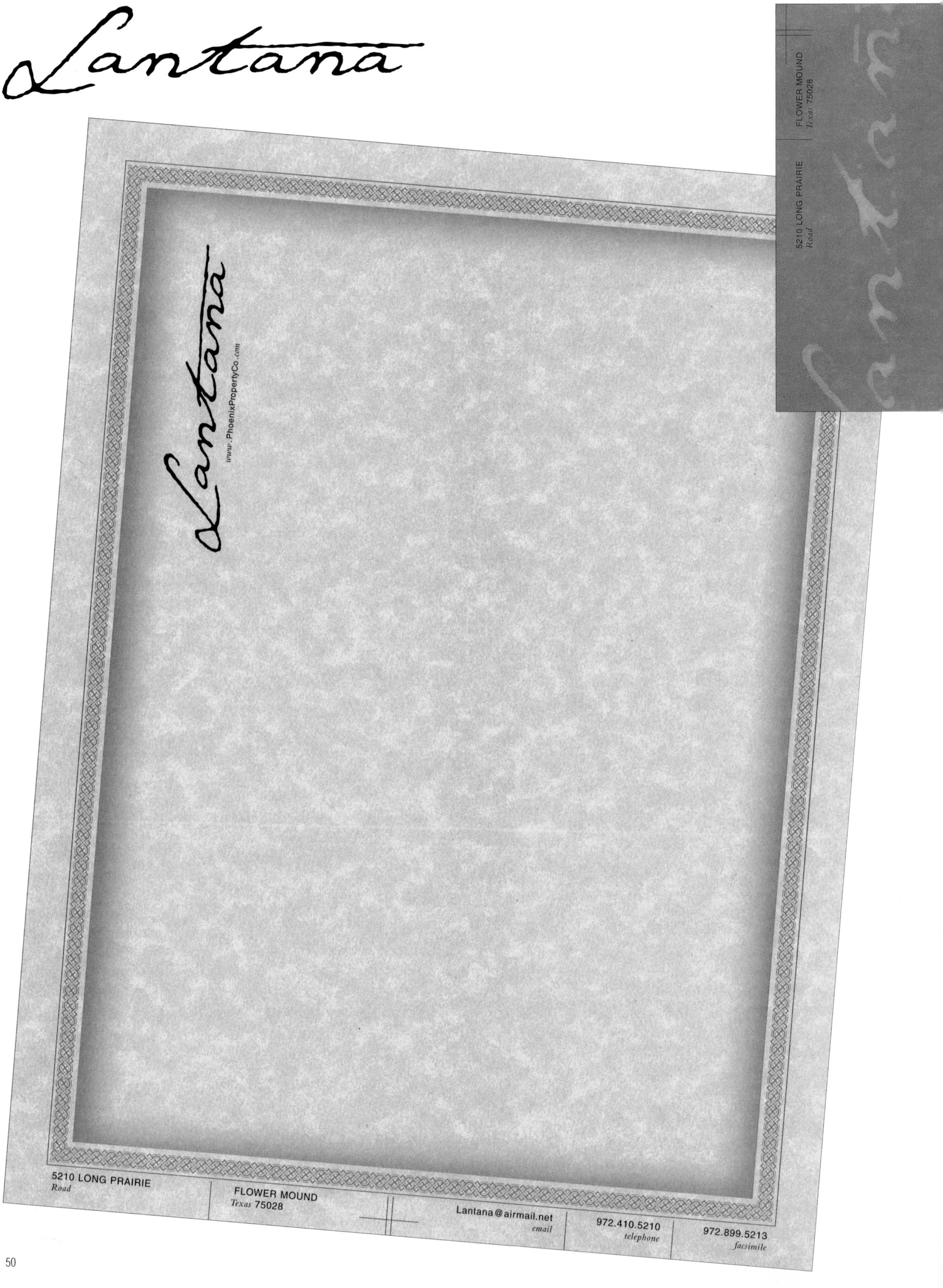

Lantana

www.PhoenixPropertyCo.com

5210 LONG PRAIRIE
Road

FLOWER MOUND
Texas 75028

Lantana@airmail.net
email

972.410.5210
telephone

972.899.5213
facsimile

5210 LONG PRAIRIE
Road

FLOWER MOUND
Texas 75028

Client
  Phoenix Property Co.
Design Firm
  VWA Group
  Dallas, Texas
Designers
  Bret Sano, Ann Thornton

Client
Executive Strategies
Design Firm
Sayles Graphic Design
Des Moines, Iowa
Art Director, Designer, Illustrator
John Sayles

Woodcliff Drive Box 22850
Rochester, NY 14692

Woodcliff Drive
Box 22850
Rochester, NY 14692

Ph. (716) 381-4000
Fax (716) 381-2673

Bob Blonowicz
Concierge
(716) 248-4807

e-Mail: bblonowicz@woodclifflodge.com
Visit us at: www.woodclifflodge.com

Resort & Conference Center

Woodcliff Drive Box 22850 Rochester, NY 14692
(716) 381-4000 Fax (716) 381-2673

e-Mail: welcome@woodclifflodge.com
Visit us at: www.woodclifflodge.com

Client
The Lodge at Woodcliff
Design Firm
**McElveney & Palozzi
Design Group, Inc.
Rochester, New York**
Creative Director
William McElveney
Art Director
Ellen Johnson

Cleo's

www.cleos.com

The Tower
2000 Las
L

0 W. Sahara Ave., #317
Vegas, Nev. 89102

Client
CLEO's
Design Firm
Tusk Studios
Las Vegas, Nevada
Designers
Debra Heiser
HTML Programming
Style Wise
Interactive

Tel: 702.242.2531 • Fax: 702.733.8160 • E-mail: inquiries@cleos.com • 3540 W. Sahara Ave., #317; Las Vegas, Nev. 89102

55

FIRESTONE
UPPER WEST SIDE

FIRESTONE
UPPER WEST SIDE

Christine Aguillard
Leasing Manager

1001 WEST SEVENTH STREET FT. WORTH, TEXAS 76102
(817) 654.2888
FAX (817) 654.2999
firestone@airmail.net

1001 WEST SEVENTH STREET FT. WORTH, TEXAS 76102
(817) 654.2888
FAX (817) 654.2999
firestone@airmail.net

1001 WEST S
STREET FT. WORTH,

FIRESTONE
UPPER WEST SIDE
A P A R T M E N T   H O M E S

FIRESTONE
UPPER WEST SIDE

FIRESTONE
UPPER WEST SIDE

1001 WEST SEVENTH STREET, FT. WORTH, TEXAS 76102

VENTH

XAS 76102

distilled images
a picture's worth

distilled images

distilled images
eighty-five bluxome san francisco california 94107

Client
Distilled Images
Design Firm
AERIAL
San Francisco, California
Designers
Tracy Moon, Misty Bralvar

distilled images
a picture's worth

eighty-five bluxome san francisco california 94107

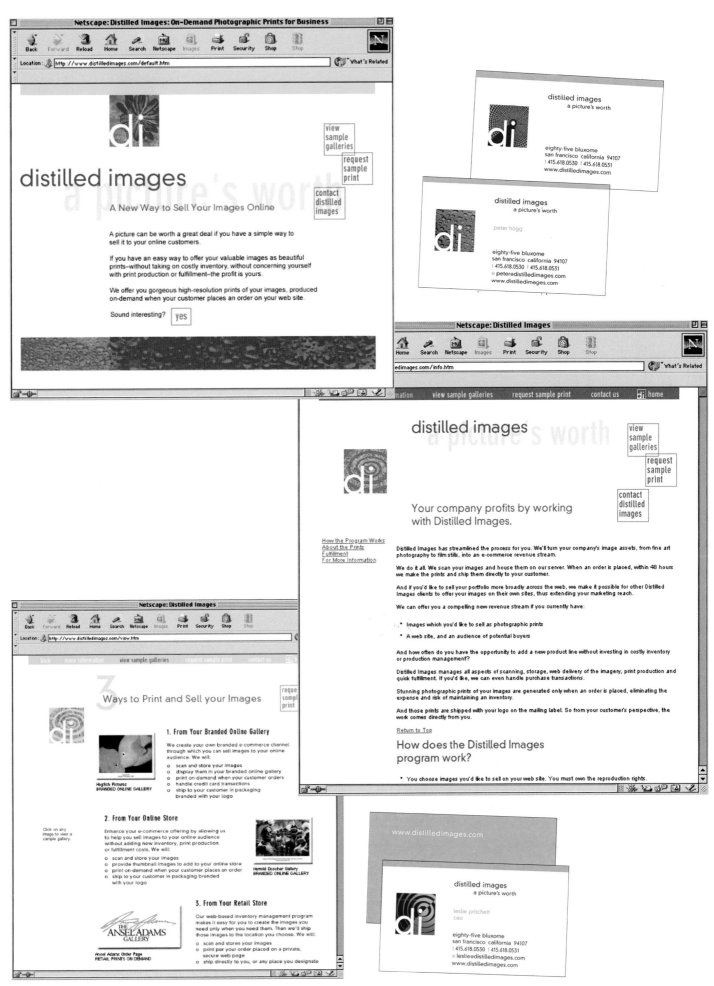

HARDWARE
· c o m ·

Client
Hardware.com
Design Firm
Hornall Anderson Design Works, Inc.
Seattle, Washington
Designers
Lisa Cerveny,
Michael Brugman, Mary Hermes

Client
The Baker Group
Design Firm
Hess Design, Inc.
Natick, Massachussetts
Designers
Kim Daly, Karyn Goba

the BAKER GROUP

Solutions for Enhancing Enrollment.

the BAKER GROUP

Solutions for Enhancing Enrollment.

54 Winthrop Street
Holliston, MA 01746
(508) 429-9178 *tel*
(508) 429-9181 *fax*

the BAKER GROUP

Solutions for Enhancing Enrollment.

54 Winthrop Street
Holliston, MA 01746

3121 Oak Orchard Road–North of Five Corners
Albion, New York 14411
(716) 589 . 8000
Fax: (716) 589 . 8001

3121 Oak Orchard Road–North of Five Corners
Albion, New York 14411

Client
Watt Farms
Country Market
Design Firm
McElveney & Palozzi
Design Group, Inc.
Rochester, New York
Creative Director
William McElveney
Art Director, Designer
Jon Westfall

 ## COUNTRY GIFT SHOP

We have a wonderful selection of gifts for all ages and occasions. You can choose from: *Mary Engelbrett Designs, Winnie the Pooh, Custom Pottery, Village Candles, Mary Meyer Plush Animals, Toland Floor Mats and Flags, Gilbertie's Natural Fragrances, Rug Barn Throws and so much more!*

HARVEST DATES:

Apricots
Mid-Late July

Nectarines
Mid August-September

Peaches
Mid July-September

Plums
Mid July-August

Apples
Late August-November

POPULAR FUDGE FLAVORS

Chocolate	*Chocolate Walnut*
Rocky Road	*Vanilla Walnut*
Maple Walnut	*Mint Chocolate Swirl*
Tiger Butter	*Peanut Butter*
Chewy Praline	*Peanut Butter Chocolate*
Penuchi Walnut	*Peanut Butter Cup*
Amaretto Swirl	*Almond Joy*

ICE CREAM SHOPPE

We serve hard ice cream and our rich vanilla and chocolate frozen custard. We also offer a no-sugar froz product as well as several no-fat yogurt and sorbet selection

Try our Turtle Sundae or a Flurry! For larger appetites, there's the *"MEGAWATT"* Sundae. Lemon and Strawber Ice have no cholesterol and are delightfully light on a ho summer day.

Have you ever had a pretzel cone? How about a chocolate chip cookie cone or a dark chocolate cookie cone? Our Ice Cream Shoppe is open through October.

3121 Oak Orchard Road
North of Five Corners
Albion, New York 14411

(716) 589 . 8000
Fax: (716) 589 . 8001
1 . 800 . 274 . 5897

Karen Watt
OWNER/OPERATOR

e-mail: kwatt@eznet.net

STREAMWORKS

STREAMWORKS

STREAMWORKS

NAME		TITLE	
Bob Caldwell		Chairman & President	

STREET	SUITE	CITY	STATE	ZIP CODE
1500 Westlake Ave. N.	118	Seattle	WA	98109-3036

PHONE	FAX	TOLL FREE
206.301.9292	206.378.1438	800.611.0008

EMAIL	INTERNET
bobca@streamworks.org	www.streamworks.org

PHONE	FAX	INTERNET	STREET	SUITE	CITY	STATE	ZIP CODE
206.301.9292	206.378.1438	www.streamworks.org	1500 Westlake Ave N	118	Seattle	WA	98109

Client
Streamworks
Design Firm
**Hornall Anderson
Design Works, Inc.
Seattle, Washington**
Designers
**Jack Anderson,
Belinda Bowling,
Andrew Smith,
Don Stayner,**

STREAMWORKS

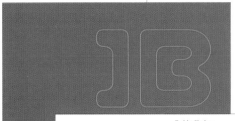

JNTELLIGENT X BIOCIDES

200 Ames Pond Drive
Tewksbury, MA 01876.9998 USA

T /   978.851.8900 x111
samsawan@ibhome.com
F /   978.851.8901

www.ibhome.com

Teddy Shalon
Chairman
T /   650.473.9190
T /   978.851.8900 x 130
tedshalon@ibhome.com
F /   650.473.9196

JNTELLIGENT X BIOCIDES

155 Island Drive
Palo Alto, CA 94301.3127 USA
www.ibhome.com

200 Ames Pond Drive
Tewksbury, MA
01876.9998 USA

JNTELLIGENT X BIOCIDES

200 Ames Pond Drive
Tewksbury, MA
01876.9998 USA

JNTELLIGENT X BIOCIDES

JNTELLIGENT X BIOCIDES

Client
   Intelligent Biocides
Design Firm
   Phoenix Creative
   St. Louis, Missouri
Designers
   Ed Mantels–Seeker

GOLD

► **FACSIMILE TRANSMITTAL**

Client
Gold & Associates
Design Firm
Gold & Associates
Ponte Vedra Beach,
Florida
Designer
Keith Gold

Company:_____

_____

Attention:_____

_____

Date:_____

Reference :_____

Fax Number:_____

Pages:_____

GOLD
► **KEITH GOLD**
President/CEO

GOLD & Associates, Inc.

Post Office Box Number 2659

Ponte Vedra Beach, Florida 32004

904-285-5669 Fax 904-285-1579

► **GOLD & Associates, Inc.**

Marketing, Design, Communications

6000-C Sawgrass Village Circle

Ponte Vedra Beach, Florida 32082

904.285.5669 Fax 904.285.1579

http://www.strikegold.com

GOLD

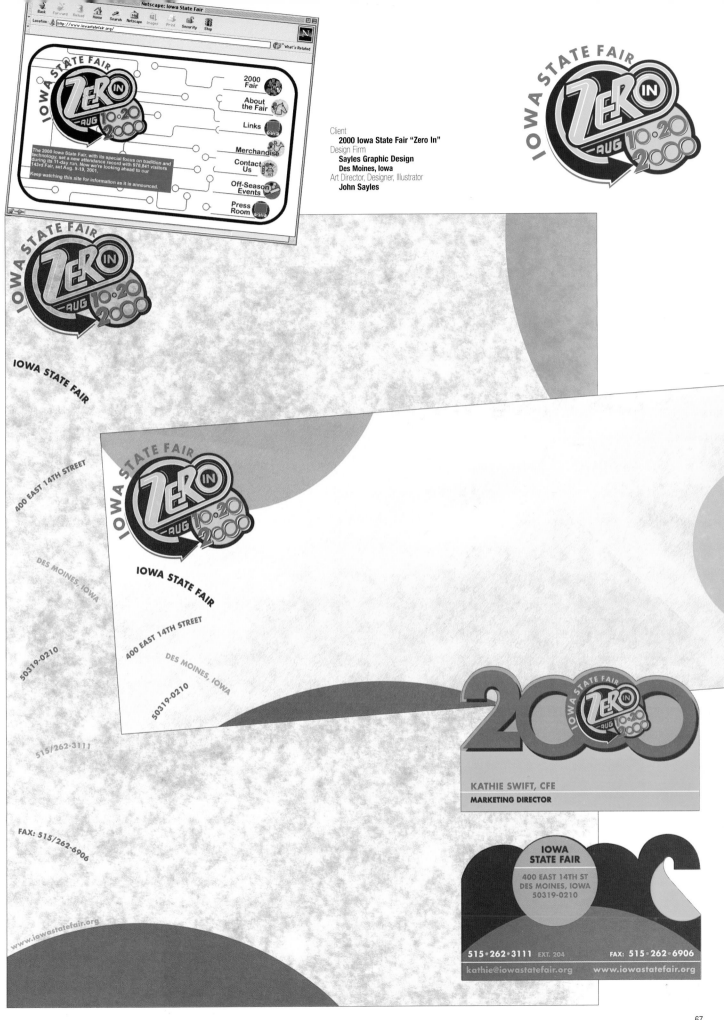

Client
2000 Iowa State Fair "Zero In"
Design Firm
Sayles Graphic Design
Des Moines, Iowa
Art Director, Designer, Illustrator
John Sayles

Client
Rocky Mountain Anglers
Design Firm
Pollman Marketing Arts, Inc.
Boulder, Colorado
Designers
Jennifer Pollman

Rocky Mountain
ANGLERS

CHIP GEORGE
ROCKY MOUNTAIN ANGLERS, INC.
2539 Pearl Street Boulder, Colorado 80302
Telephone: 303.447.2400 Facsimile: 303.447.0400 Website: www.rockymtanglers.com

ROCKY MOUNTAIN ANGLERS, INC.
2539 Pearl Street
Boulder, Colorado 80302

Rocky Mountain
ANGLERS

THE WASHINGTON
MONARCH
H O T E L

2401 M Street, N.W. Washington, D.C. 20037

THE WASHINGTON
MONARCH
HOTEL

THE WASHINGTON
MONARCH
HOTEL

Another Exceptional
Destination Hotels
& Resorts Experience

2401 M Street, N.W.   Washington, D.C.   20037   202.429.2400   Fax 202 457 5010

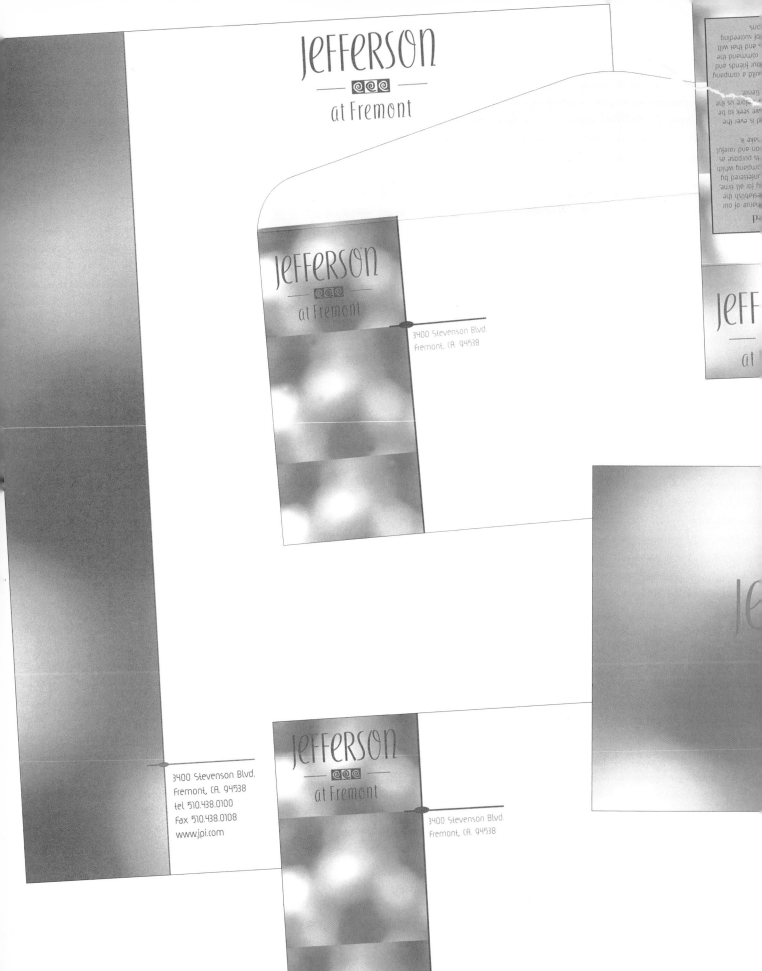

JEFFERSON
ⓒⓒⓒ
at Fremont

JEFFERSON
ⓒⓒⓒ
at Fremont

3400 Stevenson Blvd.
Fremont, CA. 94538

3400 Stevenson Blvd.
Fremont, CA. 94538
tel 510.438.0100
Fax 510.438.0108
www.jpi.com

JEFFERSON
ⓒⓒⓒ
at Fremont

3400 Stevenson Blvd.
Fremont, CA. 94538

70

JeFFerSON

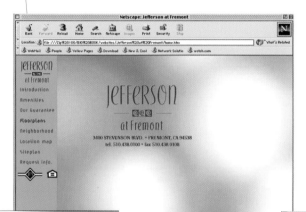

at Fremont

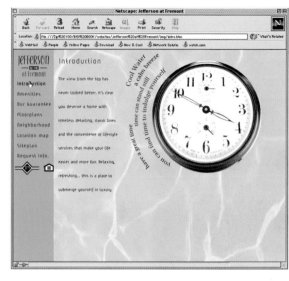

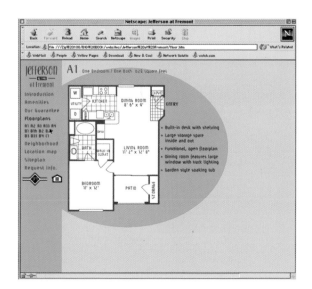

Client
JPI
Design Firm
VWA Group
Dallas, Texas
Designers
Ann Jackson, Rhonda Warren

most prints available as stock and/or fine art prints

Client
Rhea Anna Photography
Design Firm
Courage Design
Buffalo, New York
Designer
Alan Kegler

still life   portraits   toy camera   journeys

index

Still Life

Black Eyed Susan, from "Ali's Garden"

still life   portraits   toy camera   journeys

index

New Mexico

Horse and Butte

PHOTOGRAPHY

2308 Genesee St.

Buffalo, NY 14225

(716) 894-2274 *voice*

RheaCAnna@yahoo.com

www.RheaAnna.com

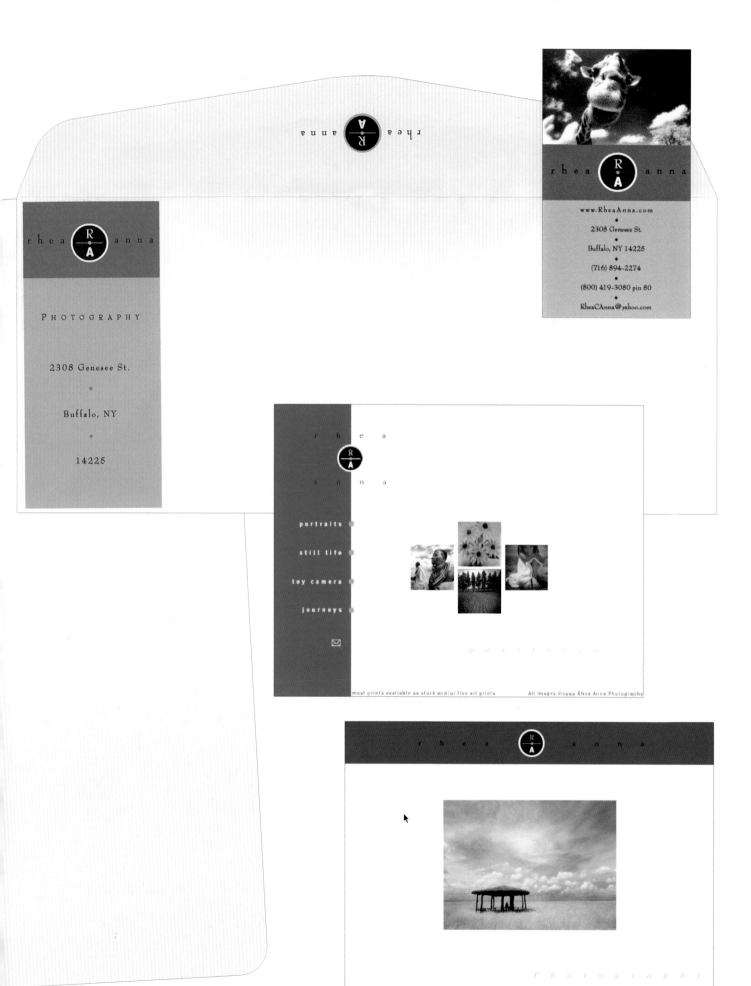

rhea anna

R
A

rhea anna

R
A

www.RheaAnna.com
•
2308 Genesee St.
•
Buffalo, NY 14225
•
(716) 894-2274
•
(800) 419-3080 pin 80
•
RheaCAnna@yahoo.com

rhea anna

R
A

PHOTOGRAPHY

2308 Genesee St.

•

Buffalo, NY

•

14225

rhea

R
A

a n n a

portraits

still life

toy camera

journeys

most prints available as stock and/or fine art prints   All images ©1999 Rhea Anna Photography

rhea   R A   anna

Photography

LOGIS LTD
9 Raffles Place
#27-01 Republic Plaza
Singapore 048619

Phone +(65) 435.0441
Fax +(65) 532.3510
askasia@logisltd.com

Client
LOGIS Ltd.
Design Firm
JOED Design Inc.
Elmhurst, Illinois
Designer
Edward Rebek

Steven P. Williams
Managing Director

LOGIS LTD
3027 Marina Bay Drive, Suite 110
League City, Texas 77573 USA
Phone +281.335.4944
Fax +281.335.3945
Mobile +44 (0) 7713.261003
Email stevewilliams@logisltd.com

a new world of global logistics has arrived | www.logisltd.com

11 Sixth Road
Woburn, MA 01801
Tel 781.932.8882
Fax 781.932.8889
info@planetpackaging.com
www.planetpackaging.com

11 Sixth Road
Woburn, MA 01801
Tel 781.932.8882
Fax 781.932.8889
www.planetpackaging.com

Client
planetpackaging.com
Design Firm
Goldforest
Miami, Florida
Designer
Ray Garcia

11 Sixth Road
Woburn, MA 01801

JEFFERSON AT
BRYAN PLACE

Client
JPI
Design Firm
VWA Group
Dallas, Texas
Designers
Rhonda Camp Warren, James Wilson

Casa Monica
H O T E L

Client
Casa Monica Hotel
Design Firm
Gold & Associates
Ponte Vedra Beach, Florida
Designer
Keith Gold

Casa Monica
HOTEL

95 Cordova Street ▾ St. Augustine, Florida 32084

Casa Monica
HOTEL

St. Augustine, Florida
1888

YOU'RE INVITED TO AN
INTRODUCTION OF

The Hudson Community Fund

WEDNESDAY, JUNE 28, 2000
HUDSON GOLF CLUB
HUDSON, WI

5:00 P.M.
REFRESHMENTS & HORS D'OEUVRES

6:00 P.M.
WELCOME & INTRODUCTION
KEN HEISER, PRESIDENT, HUDSON COMMUNITY FUND

GUEST SPEAKER
LARRY L. KATH, PRESIDENT, CEO
FOX VALLEY REGION, INC. COMMUNITY FOUNDATION

ADJOURN

BUILDING PATHWAYS
TO THE FUTURE FOR LIVING
AND GIVING

Client
**The Hudson
Community
Fund**
Design Firm
**Resco Print
Graphics
Hudson,
Wisconsin**
Designers
**Kristin Sosalla,
Barb Smothers**

P.O. BOX 943, HUDSON, WI 54016 • A DIVISION OF THE ST. CROIX VALLEY COMMUNITY FOUNDATION

BUILDING PATHWAYS TO THE FUTURE FOR LIVING AND GIVING

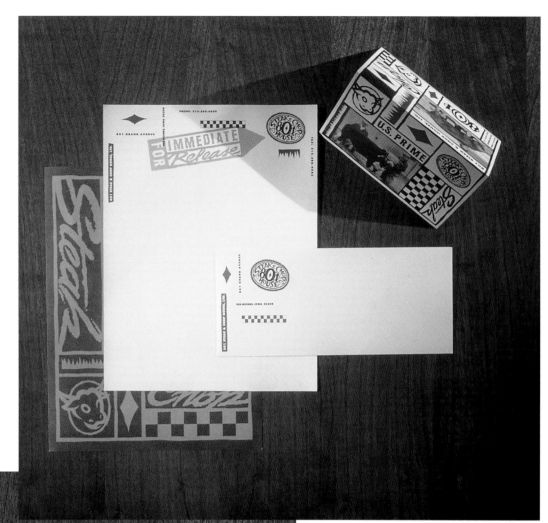

Client
801 Steak and Chop House
Design Firm
Sayles Graphic Design
Des Moines, Iowa
Art Director, Designer, Illustrator
John Sayles

Glen Ellen Carneros Winery
P.O. Box 1636 Sonoma, CA 94576 USA
Tel: 707.939.6200 Fax: 707.938.0892

Client
Glen Ellen Carneros Winery
Design Firm
Halleck
Palo Alto, California
Designers
Daniel Tang, Wayne Wright

GLEN ELLEN® IS EVERYTHING
YOU TOLD US YOU LIKE IN WINE

Charlie Tregeletos
Winemaker

Atwater Foods, INC.

Premium Dried Fruit

Your Prime Source for
DRIED FRUIT

For Over 100 Years

INNOVATIVE • RELIABLE • ACCOMMODATING

Atwater Foods, INC.

Premium Dried Fruit

Client
Atwater Foods, Inc.
Design Firm
McElveney & Palozzi Design Group Inc. Rochester, New York
Creative Director
William McElveney
Art Director, Designer
Lisa Williamson

Sulphured

The same great a
provided sulphur
browning. Comp
of Atwater dried
other and taste t

Atwater certified organic dried apples are made from apples grown by several certified growers in North America.

Additional Capabilities

Atwater Foods can provide any of the typical dried apple cuts: rings, wedges, fresh cut dices, dry cut dices and grinds. Apple fiber is also available. Both regular moisture dried (evaporated) and low moisture (dehydrated) apples are available. Specific cuts and packaging are detailed on the reverse side.

Atwater Foods, INC.

Premium Dried Fruit

10190 Route 18 Lyndonville, NY 14098 • Phone: (716) 765-2639 • (800) 836-3972 • Fax: (716) 765-9443 • www.atwaterfoods.com

Client
Tusk Studios
Design Firm
Tusk Studios
Las Vegas, Nevada
Designers
Debra Heiser,
Virginia Thompson, Scott Wizell

T H

4420 ARVILLE ST. SUITE 6
LAS VEGAS, NV 89103

4420 ARVILLE ST. SUITE 6 / LAS VEGAS, NV 89103
T: 702.257.1520 F: 702.257.2501 / www.tuskstudios.com

ILLE ST. SUITE 6
S, NV 89103
7.1520
7.2501
studios.com

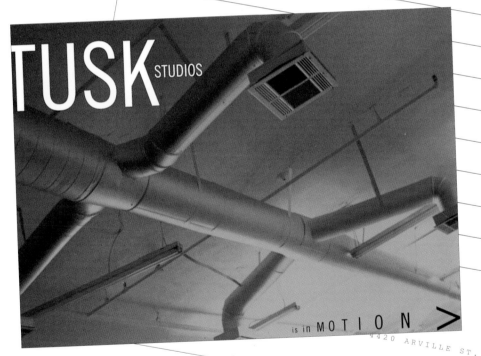

is in MOTION >

4420 ARVILLE ST. SUITE 6 / LAS VEGAS,
NV 89103
T: 702.257.1520   F: 702.257.2501 /

SCOTT WIZELL
ART DIRECTOR

4420 ARVILLE ST. SUITE 6
LAS VEGAS, NV 89103
T: 702.257.1520
F: 702.257.2501
www.tuskstudios.com

Client
Exstream
Design Firm
McDill Design
Milwaukee, Wisconsin
Designer
Brad Bedessem

WATER PURIFICATION | ENJOY THE WORLD AND DON'T WORRY ABOUT THE WATER

EXSTREAM™

ENJOY THE WORLD AND DON'T WORRY ABOUT THE WATER

123A East Wisconsin Ave.
Oconomowoc, WI 53066
Phone 262 567 5617
Facsimile 262 567 2317
www.exstreamwater.com

 Printed with soy-based ink on recycled paper.

88

Ann Moran
Vice President

123A East Wisconsin Ave.
Oconomowoc, WI 53066
Phone 262 567 5617
Cellphone 414 333 9680
Facsimile 262 567 2317
Email ann@exstreamwater.com
Website www.exstreamwater.com

EXSTREAM™

WATER TECHNOLOGIES, INC.

EXSTREAM WATER TECHNOLOGIES, INC.
123A East Wisconsin Ave.
Oconomowoc, WI 53066

Client
Cantilever Technologies
Design Firm
Maddock Douglas, Inc.
Elmhurst, Illinois
Designer
Maddock Douglas

JULIE K. GOONEWARDENE
PRESIDENT

FROM APPROACH TO EXECUTION™

PURDUE TECHNOLOGY CENTER · 3000 KENT AVENUE · WEST LAFAYETTE, INDIANA 47906
EMAIL: JGOONEWARDENE@CANTILEVERTECH.COM · PHONE: 765.775.4552 · FAX: 765.496.6489

FROM APPROACH TO EXECUTION™

PURDUE TECHNOLOGY CENTER · 3000 KENT AVENUE · WEST LAFAYETTE, INDIANA 47906

Una Daniels-Edwards

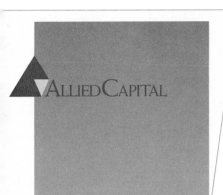

1919 Pennsylvania Avenue NW
Washington, DC 20006-3434
202.721.1817
fax 202.659.2053
uedwards@alliedcapital.com

Client
Allied Capital
Design Firm
Greenfield/Belser Ltd.
Washington, D.C.
Designer
Burkey Belser

1919 Pennsylvania Avenue NW
Washington, DC 20006-3434
202.331.1112
fax 202.659.2053

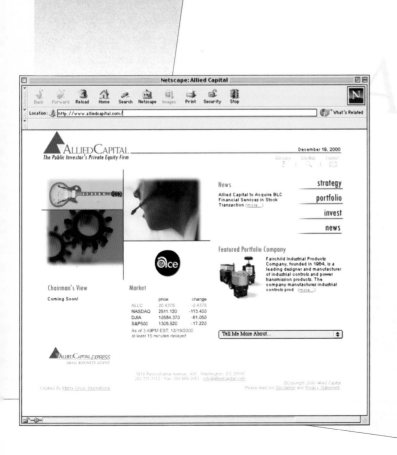

134

ARCH

STREET

★

PHILADELPHIA

PENNSYLVANIA

19106

134
ARCH
STREET
★
PHILADELPHIA, PA
19106
★
TELEPHONE
215·440·9166
FAX
215·440·0793

134

ARCH

STREET

★

PHILADELPHIA

PENNSYLVANIA

19106

★

TELEPHONE

215·440·9166

FAX

215·440·0793

Client
Old Market Street
Design Firm
Randi Wolf Design
Glassboro, New Jersey
Designer
Randi Wolf

LYNN MARTIN HASKIN, PH.D.
CHAIRMAN

134 ARCH STREET
★
PHILADELPHIA, PA
19106
★

TELEPHONE
215·440·9166
FAX
215·440·0793

AL FAISALIAH HOTEL
RIYADH, SAUDI ARABIA

ROSEWOOD HOTELS & RESORTS

Client
Rosewood Hotels
Design Firm
VWA Group
Dallas, Texas
Designer
Rhonda Camp Warren

AL FAISALIAH HOTEL
RIYADH, SAUDI ARABIA

ROSEWOOD HOTELS & RESORTS

فندق الفيصلية

AL FAISALIAH HOTEL

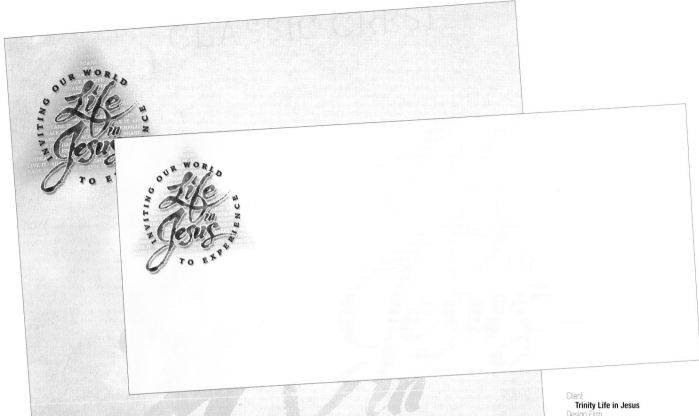

Client
Trinity Life in Jesus
Design Firm
Dotzler Creative Arts
Omaha, Nebraska

🔥 TRINITY CHURCH
INTERDENOMINATIONAL

15555 West Dodge Road • Omaha, Nebraska 68154-2070 • Phone (402) 330-5724 • FAX (402) 330-2084 • www.trinityomaha.com

585 Hinano Street, Hilo, Hawaii 96720

CANDIES
BIG ISLAND™

Client
  Big Island Candies
Design Firm
  Hornall Anderson Design Works, Inc.
  Seattle, Washington
Designers
  Jack Anderson, Kathy Saito,
  Alan Copeland, Mary Chin Hutchison

CANDIES
BIG ISLAND™

CANDIES
BIG ISLAND™

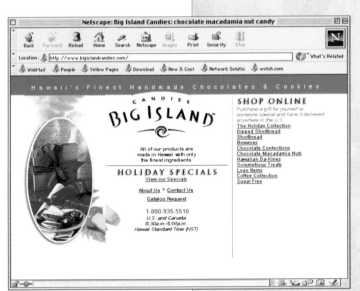

Netscape: Big Island Candies: chocolate macadamia nut candy

Back Forward Reload Home Search Netscape Images Print Security Stop

Location: http://www.bigislandcandies.com/

WebMail   People   Yellow Pages   Download   New & Cool   Network Solutio   wotch.com

Hawaii's Finest Handmade Chocolates & Cookies

CANDIES
BIG ISLAND™

All of our products are
made in Hawaii with only
the finest ingredients

HOLIDAY SPECIALS
View our Specials

About Us • Contact Us
Catalog Request

1-800-935-5510
U.S. and Canada
6:30a.m.-5:00p.m.
Hawaii Standard Time (HST)

SHOP ONLINE
Purchase a gift for yourself or
someone special and have it delivered
anywhere in the U.S.
The Holiday Collection
Dipped Shortbread
Shortbread
Brownies
Chocolate Confections
Chocolate Macadamia Nuts
Hawaiian Da-Kines
Scrumptious Treats
Logo Items
Coffee Collection
Sugar Free

CANDIES
BIG ISLAND™

585 Hinano Street
Hilo, Hawaii 96720
Retail: 1.808.935.8890
1.800.935.5510
f. 808.961.0659

www.bigislandcandies.com

585 Hinano Street   Hilo, Hawaii 96720   t 808.961.2199   f 808.961.6941   Retail: 1.800.935.5510   f 808.961.0659   www.bigislandcandies.com

Client
Fly Graphics
Design Firm
Fly Graphics
Richmond, Kentucky
Designer
Frank L. Yates

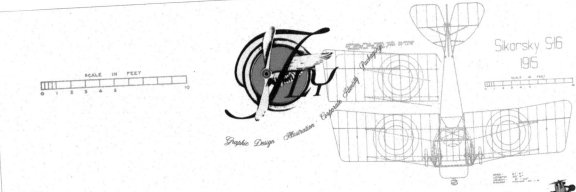

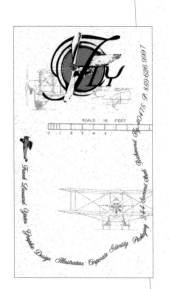

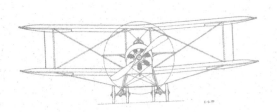

Larry Kline
Software Engineer

944 Market Street, Suite 403
San Francisco, CA 94102

415/369.0360

larry.kline@epropose.com

www.epropose.com

Client
   epropose
Design Firm
   Hunt Weber Clark Assoc., Inc.
   San Francisco, California
Designers
   Nancy Hunt-Weber, Jason Bell

e **propose**

e **propose**

944 Market Street, Suite 403
San Francisco, CA 94102

944 Market Street, Suite 403 • San Francisco,
Phone 415/369.0360 • **E-mail** info@epropose.com • **We**

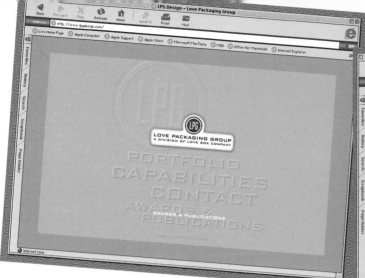

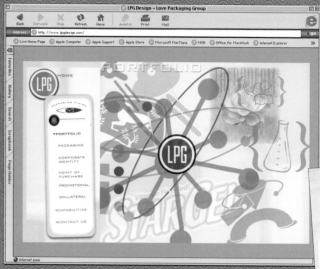

LOVE PACKAGING GROUP
A DIVISION OF LOVE BOX COMPANY

410 EAST 37TH STREET NORTH
WICHITA, KANSAS 67219-3556

LOVE PACKAGING GROUP
A DIVISION OF LOVE BOX COMPANY

CHRIS WEST
CREATIVE DIRECTOR

TEL 316-832-3203

LOVE PACKAGING GROUP
A DIVISION OF LOVE BOX COMPANY

Client
Love Packaging Group
Design Firm
Love Packaging Group
Wichita, Kansas
Designers
**Chris West, Rick Gimlin,
Lorna West, Dustin Commer**

www.LPGdesign.com

410 EAST 37TH STREET NORTH
WICHITA, KANSAS 67219-3556
TEL 316-832-3229 • FAX 316-832-3293

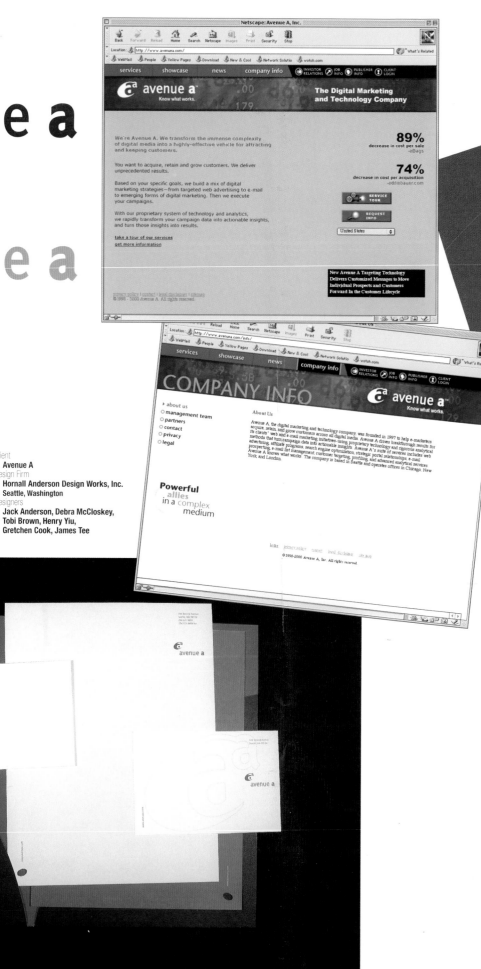

Client
Avenue A
Design Firm
Hornall Anderson Design Works, Inc.
Seattle, Washington
Designers
Jack Anderson, Debra McCloskey,
Tobi Brown, Henry Yiu,
Gretchen Cook, James Tee

avenue a

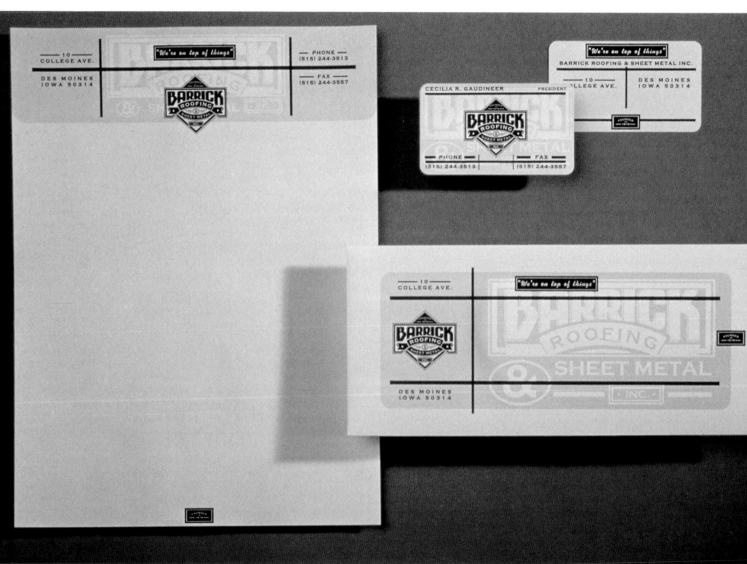

Client
Barrick Roofing
Design Firm
Sayles Graphic Design
Des Moines, Iowa
Art Director, Designer, Illustrator
John Sayles

Client
Surfacine Consumer Products
Design Firm
Phoenix Creative
St. Louis, Missouri
Designer
Ed Mantels-Seeker

Surfacine
Consumer Products LLC

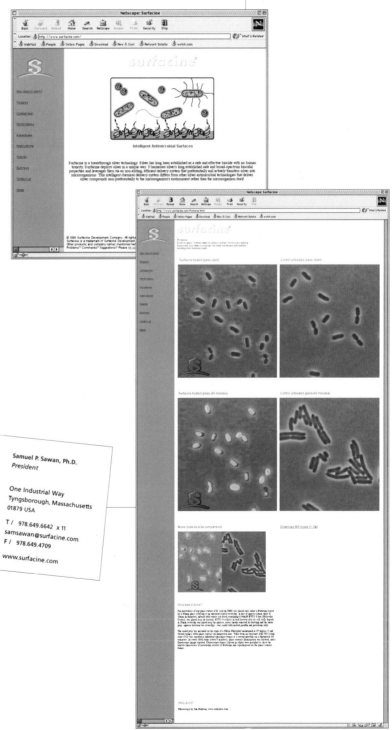

surfacine®

Samuel P. Sawan, Ph.D.
President

One Industrial Way
Tyngsborough, Massachusetts
01879 USA

T / 978.649.6642 x 11
samsawan@surfacine.com
F / 978.649.4709

www.surfacine.com

The Vein Center

Client
The Vein Center
Design Firm
Kiku Obata and Company
St. Louis, Missouri
Designer
Ed Mantels-Seeker

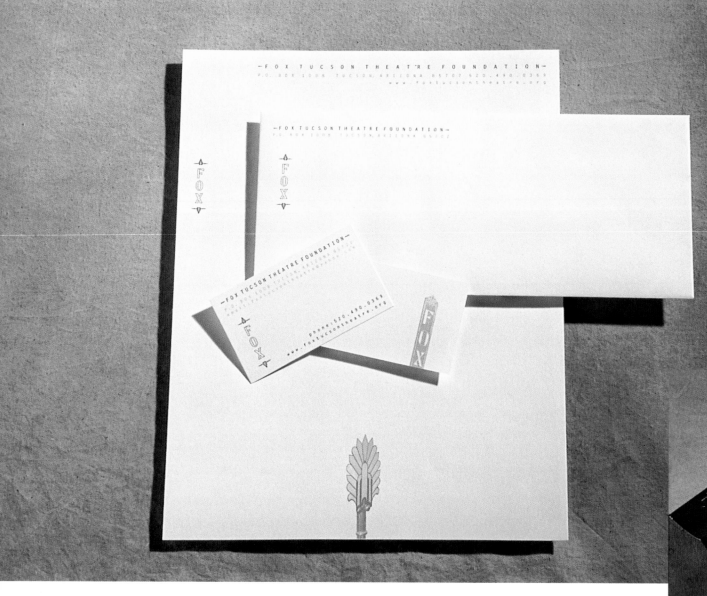

Client
Fox Theatre Tucson
Design Firm
Boelts Bros. Associates
Tucson, Arizona
Designers
K. Stratford, J. Boelts, E. Boelts

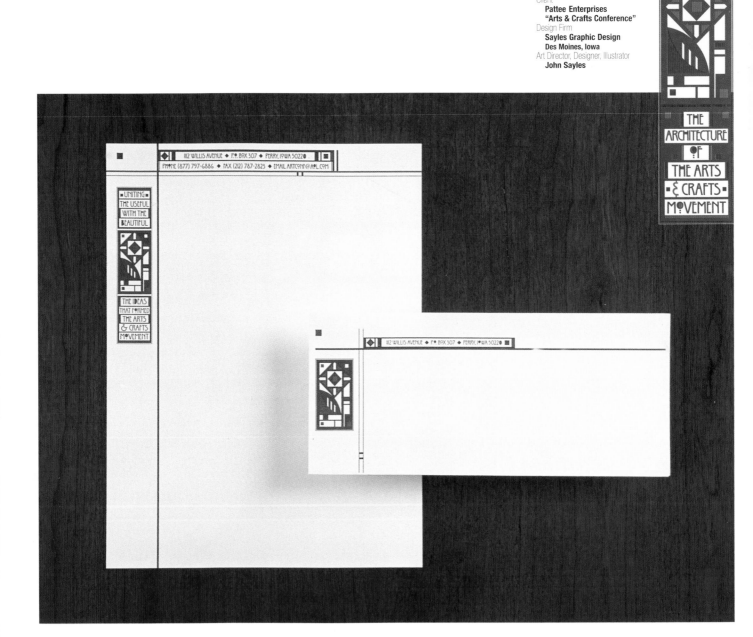

Client
Pattee Enterprises
"Arts & Crafts Conference"
Design Firm
Sayles Graphic Design
Des Moines, Iowa
Art Director, Designer, Illustrator
John Sayles

TRINITY PROJECT
A Church For The Northwest

We intend to be a creative church that grows by consistently providing a safe place for Northwesterners to discover and grow in authentic Christian spirituality through special events, contemporary worship and diverse small groups.

TRINITY PROJECT
Church For The Northwest

TRINITY PROJECT
A Church For The Northwest

Ron Hockley
Director

16409 SE Division, Suite 318 • Portland, OR 97236
Phone/Fax: 503/ 492-2040 • e-mail: RHockley@aol.com

Client
Trinity Project
Design Firm
Jeff Fisher LogoMotives
Portland, Oregon
Designer
Jeff Fisher

TRINITY PROJECT
A Church For The Northwest
16409 SE Division, Suite 318
Portland, Oregon 97236

9 SE Division, Suite 318
and, Oregon 97236
e/Fax: **503/ 492-2040**

NIDUS™
CENTER FOR SCIENTIFIC ENTERPRISE

Client
Monsanto Company/Nidus Center
Design Firm
Phoenix Creative
St. Louis, Missouri
Designer
Ed Mantels-Seeker

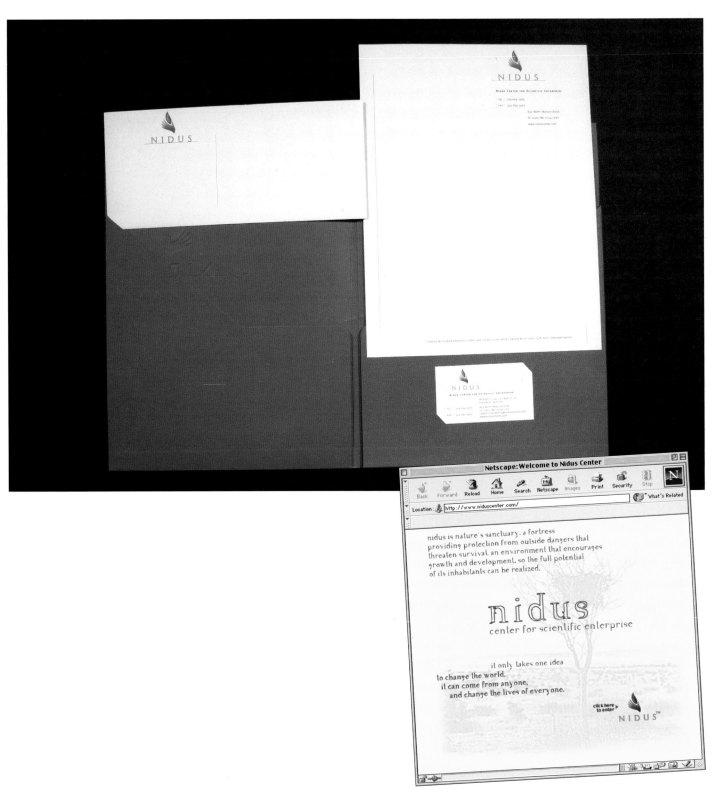

RECHARGE

Client
Recharge
Design Firm
**Hornall Anderson
Design Works, Inc.
Seattle, Washington**
Designers
**Jack Anderson,
Katha Dalton,
Henry Yiu,
Tiffany Scheiblauer,
Darlin Gray,
Brad Sherman,
Heidi Favour,
Alan Florsheim**

114

RECHARGE®
A Division of The Bamford Group, Inc.

18512
NE 19th Place
First Floor
Bellevue, WA
98008

t 425.747.7300
f 425.747.1687
w www.rechargenow.com

Client
Iowa State Fair Blue Ribbon Foundation
"Corndog Kickoff"
Design Firm
Sayles Graphic Design
Des Moines, Iowa
Art Director, Designer, Illustrator
John Sayles

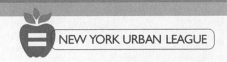

CENTRAL OFFICE:
New York Urban League, Inc.
204 West 136th Street
New York, NY 10030

TEL: 212 926 8000
FAX: 212 283 2736

www.nyul.org

BOARD OF DIRECTORS

OFFICERS

Chairman
Jonathan Rinehart
Senior Vice Chairman
Elizabeth D. Moore
Vice Chairman
David W. Sussman
Secretary
Jeff Burns, Jr.
Assistant Secretary
Noel N. Hankin
Treasurer
Paul Facella
Assistant Treasurer
Douglas P. Lawrence
General Counsel
Michael F. Armstrong
President and
Chief Executive Officer
Dennis M. Walcott

BOARD MEMBERS
Douglas X. Alexander
Alvin L. Bragg, Jr.
Alfonso L. Carney, Jr.
Dolly Christian
Larry Dais
Michelle C. Donaldson
Paul E. Gibson
Monique Greenwood
Phyllis Hodges
Jean-Marie Horovitz
Mrs. Theodore W. Kheel*
Hon. E. Leo Milonas
John D. McCain
Richard McEachern
Glenda McNeal
Harvey I. Newman
William Radinson
Rita Robinson
Michelle Rodney
Paul M. Rumely
Ida B. Smith
Elinor Tatum
Earl T. Teasley
Todd M. Turner
Jan R. Van Meter

* Honorary Director

Dennis M. Walcott
President and Chief Executive Officer

TEL: 212 926 8000 EXT. 17	New York Urban League, Inc.
FAX: 212 283 2736	204 West 136th Street
nyuldw@aol.com	New York, NY 10030

CENTRAL OFFICE:
New York Urban League, Inc.
204 West 136th Street
New York, NY 10030

www.nyul.org

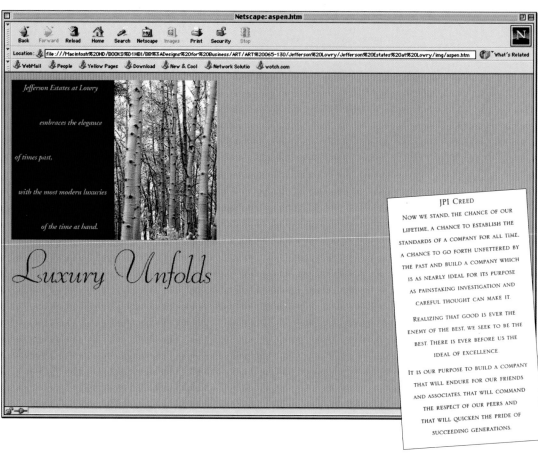

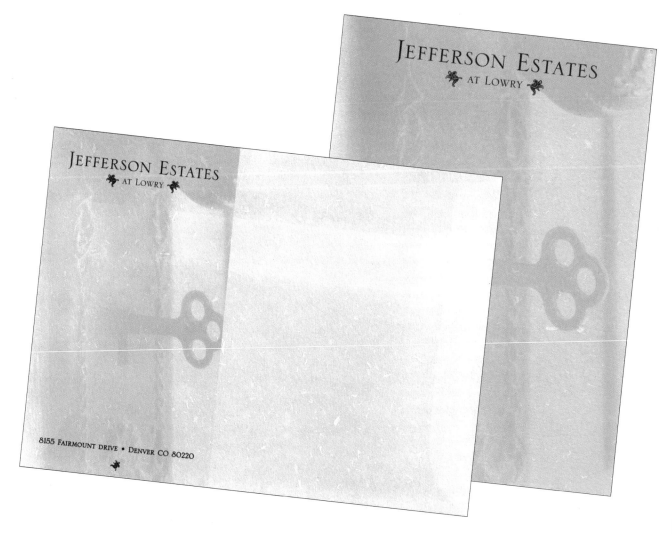

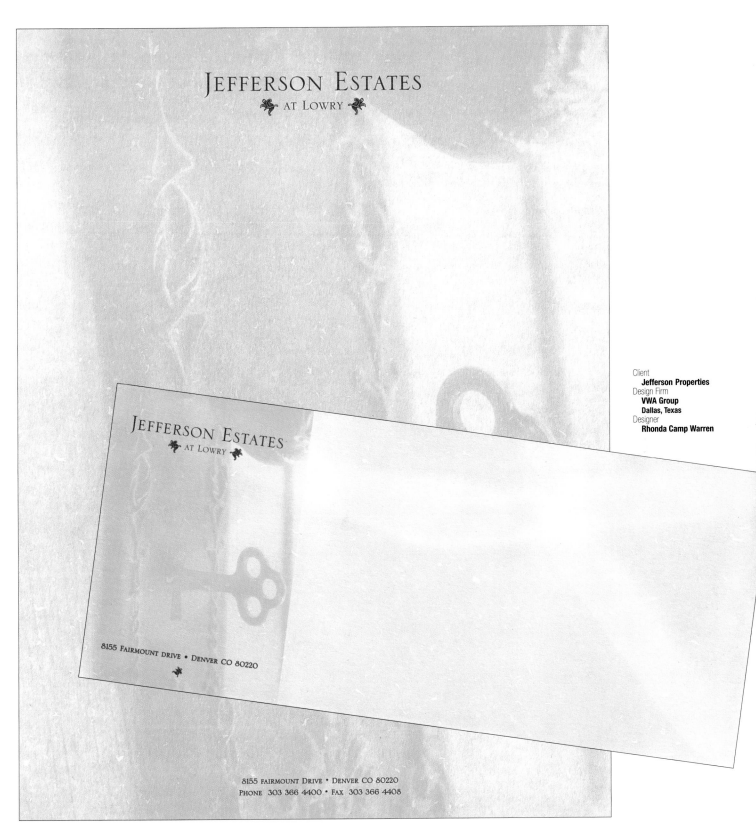

Client
Jefferson Properties
Design Firm
VWA Group
Dallas, Texas
Designer
Rhonda Camp Warren

CLAYTON CHAMBER OF COMMERCE

Up-to-date information on Businesses, Schools, Realtors, Hotels, Restaurants and much more

CLAYTON CHAMBER OF COMMERCE

RELOCATION Guide

Clayton, Missouri

CLAYTON CHAMBER OF COMMERCE

225 South Meramec Ave.
Suite 300
Clayton, Missouri 63105
314-726-3033 Fax 726-0637
website:
www.claytonmochamber.org

Lisa J. O'Brien
Executive Director

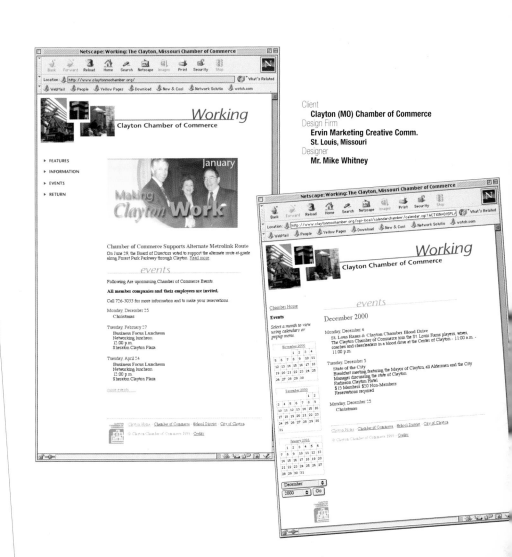

3750 S. Corona St.
Englewood, CO 80110

Kay Johnson

*Keynotes with music
to unlock the song
in your heart.*

3750 S. Corona St. • Englewood, CO 80110
(303) 809-9959 • Fax: (303) 761-8256
www.kaysingsout.com • kay@kaysingsout.com

Client
Kay Johnson's Sing Out Productions
Design Firm
Jeff Fisher LogoMotives
Portland, Oregon
Designer, Website Consultant
Jeff Fisher
Website Designer
Jason Reynolds

3750 S. Corona St.
Englewood, CO 80110

(303) 809-9959
Fax: (303) 761-8256

www.kaysingsout.com
kay@kaysingsout.com

Meena Mirshab Keuer

MASTERPRINT

3400 INDUSTRIAL LANE #2

BROOMFIELD, COLORADO 80020

TEL: 303 . 466 . 1800

FAX: 303 . 438 . 8454

http://www.masterprnt.com

QUALITY PRINTING SOLUTIONS

MASTERPRINT

3400 INDUSTRIAL LANE #2

BROOMFIELD

COLORADO 80020

TEL: 303 . 466 . 1800

FAX: 303 . 438 . 8454

http://www.masterprnt.com

Client
  Masterprint
Design Firm
  **Pollman Marketing
  Arts, Inc.**
  Boulder, Colorado
Designer
  Jennifer Pollman

MAYER BROS.
— Since 1852 —

FINE BEVERAGES

Client
Mayer Bros.
Design Firm
McElveney & Palozzi
Design Group Inc.
Rochester, New York
Creative Director
William McElveney
Art Director
Lisa Parenti

3300 Transit Road, West Seneca, New York 14224
716.668.1787 Fax 716.668.2437

My Grandfather, Jacob Mayer
founded the family business in 1852.
Today Mayer Bros. remains a
privately held company, providing
fine beverages from multiple
processing facilities to a growing
network of National Accounts.
Through four generations our
beverage offerings have grown to
include Spring Water, Fruit Juices
and Apple Cider.

Client
Jacksonville Jazz Festival • WJCT
Design Firm
Gold & Associates
Ponte Vedra Beach, Florida
Designer
Keith Gold

100 Festival Park Avenue • Jacksonville, FL 32202-1397

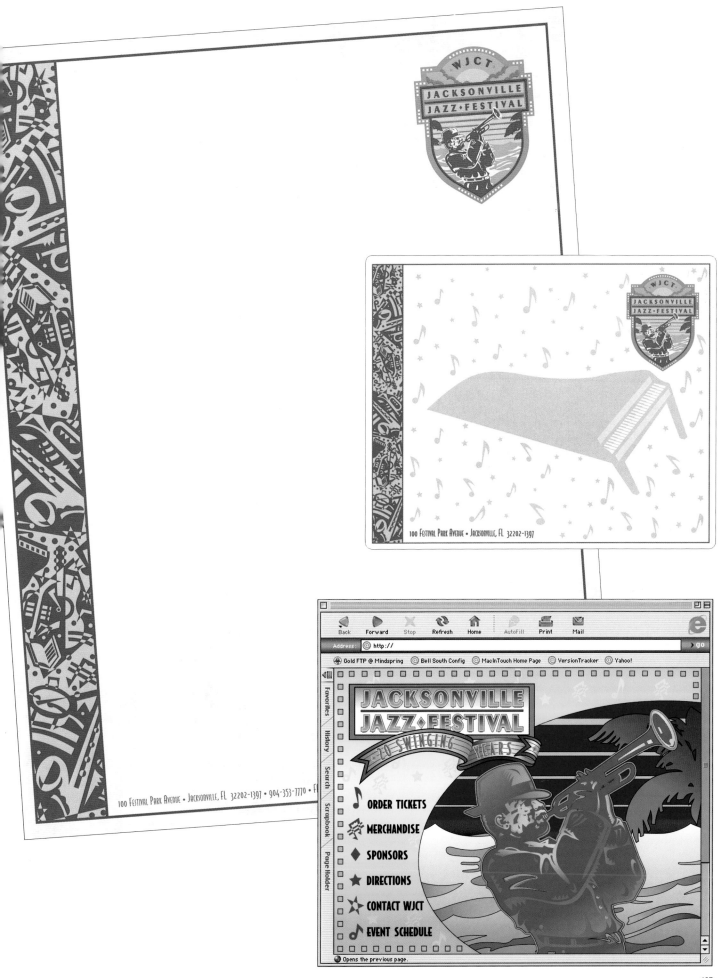

100 FESTIVAL PARK AVENUE • JACKSONVILLE, FL 32202-1397 • 904-353-7770 • F

100 Festival Park Avenue • Jacksonville, FL 32202-1397

JACKSONVILLE JAZZ • FESTIVAL
20 SWINGING YEARS

♪ ORDER TICKETS

✦ MERCHANDISE

◆ SPONSORS

★ DIRECTIONS

✦ CONTACT WJCT

♪ EVENT SCHEDULE

Address: http://   › go

Gold FTP @ Mindspring   Bell South Config   MacInTouch Home Page   VersionTracker   Yahoo!

Back   Forward   Stop   Refresh   Home   AutoFill   Print   Mail

Favorites History Search Scrapbook Page Holder

Opens the previous page.

Client
bHive
Design Firm
Bjornson Design Associates, Inc.
Philadelphia, Pennsylvania
Designer
Jon Anders Bjornson

GeoTrust ℠

Client
GeoTrust
Design Firm
Belyea
Seattle, Washington
Art Director
Patricia Belyea
Designer
Ron Lars Hansen

Sutherland
Asbill &
Brennan LLP
ATTORNEYS AT LAW

Sutherland
Asbill &
Brennan LLP
ATTORNEYS AT LAW

Sutherland
Asbill &
Brennan LLP
ATTORNEYS AT LAW

1275 Pennsylvania Avenue, NW
Washington, DC 20004-2415

Sutherland
Asbill &
Brennan LLP
ATTORNEYS AT LAW

W. Mark Smith

202.383.0221
msmith@sablaw.com

1275 Pennsylvania Avenue, NW
Washington, DC 20004-2415
202.637.3593 fax

Atlanta   ▪   Austin   ▪   New York

Sutherland Asbill & Brennan LLP
ATTORNEYS AT LAW

onal focus

hal perspective

Client
Sutherland Asbill & Brennan LLP
Design Firm
Greenfield/Belser Ltd.
Washington, D.C.
Designers
Burkey Belser, Kim Bieler

131

Client
Big Daddy Photography
Design Firm
Sayles Graphic Design
Des Moines, Iowa
Art Director, Designer, Illustrator
John Sayles

Client
Kimpton Hotel + Restaurant Group
Design Firm
Hunt Weber Clark Assoc., Inc.
San Francisco, California
Designers
Nancy Hunt-Weber,
Leigh Krichbaum

SERRANO HOTEL
SAN FRANCISCO

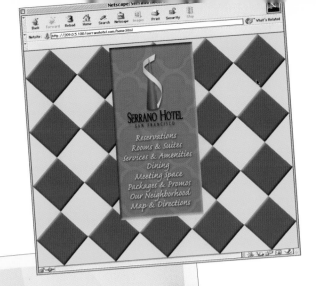

A R T I S A N P A R T N E R S

A R T I S A N P A R T N E R S L I M I T E D P A R T N E R S H I P

ARTISAN FUNDS

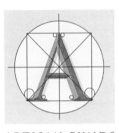

ARTISAN FUNDS

Enclosed Is The Information You Requested
On The **Artisan Small Cap Fund**...

Investment Management Practiced with Intelligence and Discipline is an Art

1·800·344·1770

Client
Artisan Partners
Design Firm
McDill Design
Milwaukee, Wisconsin
Designer
Brad Bedessem

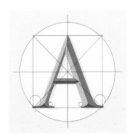

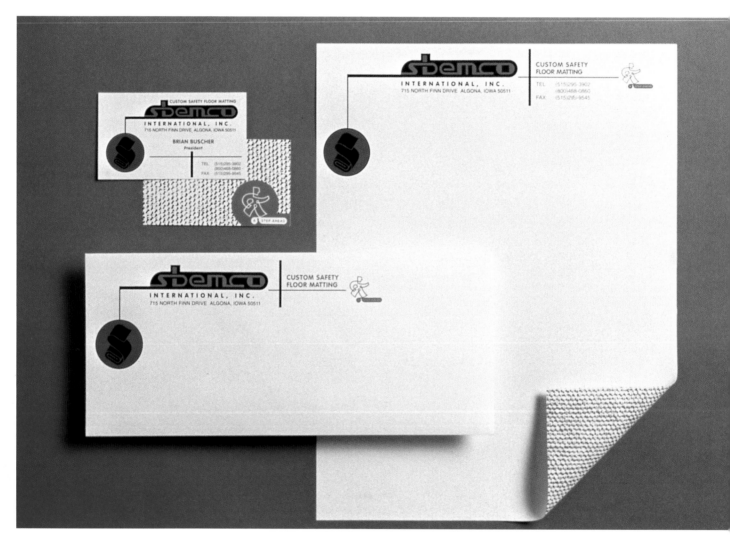

Client
Sbemco International
Design Firm
Sayles Graphic Design
Des Moines, Iowa
Art Director, Designer, Illustrator
John Sayles

FACSIMILE

Date:

Company:

Fax Number:

Attention:

Project:

Project Number:

For Your Use:

Approval:

Correct & Return:

Sign & Return:

Total Pages w/ Cover:

SHIMOKOCHI/REEVES
STRATEGIC VISUAL BRANDING

SHIMOKOCHI/REEVES
IDENTITY & PACKAGE DESIGN CONSULTANTS
4465 WILSHIRE BLVD #305
LOS ANGELES CA 90010-3704

Client
Shimokochi/Reeves
Design Firm
Shimokochi/Reeves
Los Angeles, California
Designers
Mamoru Shimokochi,
Anne Reeves

SHIMOKOCHI/REEVES
IDENTITY & PACKAGE DESIGN CONSULTANTS
4465 WILSHIRE BLVD #305
LOS ANGELES CA 90010-3704
TEL: 323·937·3414
FAX: 323·937·3417

SHIMOKOCHI/REEVES
IDENTITY & PACKAGE DESIGN CONSULTANTS
4465 WILSHIRE BLVD #305
LOS ANGELES CA 90010-3704
TEL: 323·937·3414
FAX: 323·937·3417
e-mail: shimoreeve@earthlink.net

ANNE REEVES
VICE PRESIDENT/DIRECTOR OF MARKETING

Client
Witlyn Homes
Design Firm
Artworks Advertising
Killeen, Texas
Designer
Keith Dotson

WITLYN HOMES

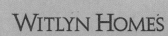

WITLYN HOMES

Larry Witten
President

P.O. Box 1994
Temple, Texas 76503-1994

(254) 742-1888   Phone/Fax
(254) 760-7980   Mobile
larry@witlynhomes.com E-mail

P.O. Box 1994 • Temple, Texas 76503-1994
(254) 742-1888•Phone/Fax

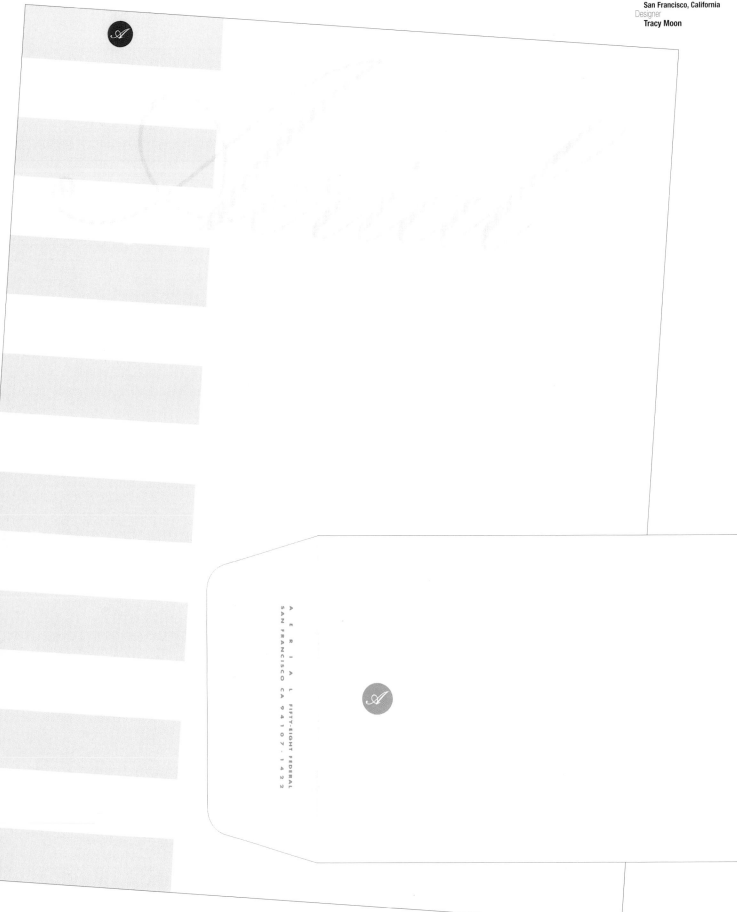

Client
AERIAL
Design Firm
AERIAL
San Francisco, California
Designer
Tracy Moon

Facsimile

(caution: this transmission is a mere facsimile of the original)

DATE:

TO:

CC:

FROM:

REGARDING:

TOTAL # OF PAGES:

A E R I A L FIFTY-EIGHT FEDERAL
SAN FRANCISCO CA 94107 - 1422

AERIAL 58 FEDERAL SAN FRANCISCO, CA 94107 TEL 415 957 9761 FAX 957 9739

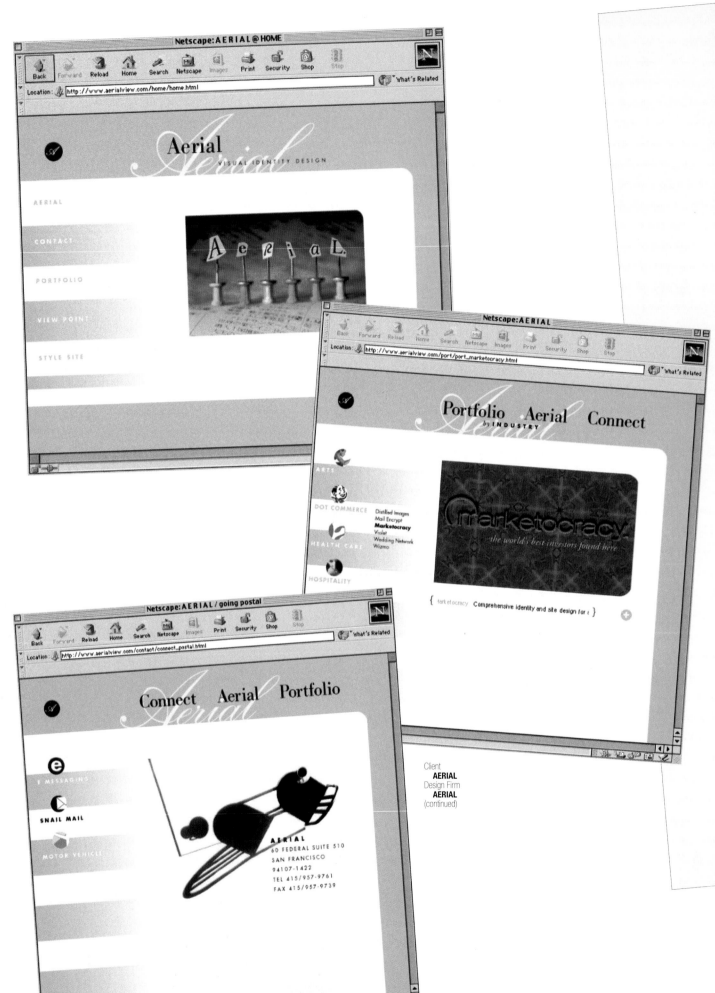

Client
AERIAL
Design Firm
AERIAL
(continued)

Client Request Form

DATE:

TO:

FROM:

PROJECT INFORMATION
(Please attach any copy, data, examples, schedules, information, etc. which will aid in the accurate estimation and/or completion of the project. Be sure to include answers to all of the relevant questions listed below.)

Project Name:

Project Type: (Check one)   ○ New   ○ Change of Scope *(to existing project)*

Final Art to be Supplied as: (Check one)   ○ Disk   ○ Film   ○ Printed/Fabricated

Date Due:

Brief Description:

Copy Provided to Aerial?   ○ Yes   ○ No   If Yes, Date Ready:

Quantity Needed: (if applicable)

Other:
(Please list any budget considerations, production issues, etc. that we should know before beginning design)

CONTACT INFORMATION
(Please list name and telephone number of key personnel for this project)

Primary:

Secondary:

Billing: (payment/invoices to)

IMPORTANT: PROJECT CONTENT AND PERTINENT SUPPORT MATERIAL MUST BE INCLUDED WITH THIS REQUEST IN ORDER FOR AERIAL'S ESTIMATE AND/OR WORK TO BE ACCURATE & TIMELY. ANY CHANGES OF SCOPE WILL BE BILLED ON AN HOURLY BASIS AT THE RATES OUTLINED IN THE ORIGINAL PROJECT PROPOSAL UNLESS COVERED BY SEPARATE WRITTEN ESTIMATE/AGREEMENT. PLEASE CALL IF YOU HAVE ANY QUESTIONS ABOUT ANY DESIGN/PRINT REQUEST WITH US PRIOR TO COMPLETION AND SUBMISSION OF THIS REQUEST FORM. THANKS!

A E R I A L   58 FEDERAL   SAN FRANCISCO   94107-1422   TEL 415 957 9761   FAX 957 9739

Client
Hotel Fort Des Moines
Design Firm
Sayles Graphic Design
Des Moines, Iowa
Art Director, Designer, Illustrator
John Sayles

the GABRIEL *Consortium, inc.*

Client
The Gabriel Consortium, Inc.
Design Firm
Dever Designs
Laurel, Maryland
Designer
Jeffrey L. Dever

the GABRIEL *Consortium, inc.*

the GABRIEL *Consortium, inc.*

13004 Brookmill Court, Laurel, Maryland 20708-2350

ROBERT H. PRATT
Media Specialist

the GABRIEL *Consortium, inc.*

13004 Brookmill Court
Laurel, Maryland 20708-2350
Tel. 301·776·3130
Fax 301·776·4854

13004 Brookmill Court, Laurel, Maryland 20708-2350 • Tel. 301·776·3130 • Fax 301·776·4854

The **SHAW** Center
FOR AESTHETIC ENHANCEMENT, LTD.

Client
The Shaw Center
Design Firm
Sullivan Marketing & Communications
Phoenix, Arizona
Designer
Jack Sullivan

Lawrence W. Shaw, M.D.
Plastic and Reconstructive Surgery

MEMBER
American Society of
Plastic and Reconstructive Surgeons, Inc.

9522 East San Salvador Drive
Suite 301
Scottsdale, AZ
85258

Tel: 480.767.1900
Fax: 480.767.0493
Email: info@theshawcenter.com
www.theshawcenter.com

The **SHAW** Center
FOR AESTHETIC ENHANCEMENT, LTD.

9522 E. San Salvador Dr
Suite 301
Scottsdale, AZ
85258

The **SHAW** Center
FOR AESTHETIC ENHANCEMENT, LTD.

Lawrence W. Shaw, M.D.
Plastic and Reconstructive Surgery

Date _____ At _____ M T W T F

Date _____ At _____ M T W T F

Date _____ At _____ M T W T F

9522 E. San Salvador Dr.

Suite 301

Scottsdale, AZ

85258

Tel: 480.767.1900

Fax: 480.767.0493

The SHAW Center
FOR AESTHETIC ENHANCEMENT, LTD.

Lawrence W. Shaw, M.D.
Plastic and Reconstructive Surgery

www.theshawcenter.com

Lawrence W. Shaw, M.D.
www.theshawcenter.com

Lawrence W. Shaw, M.D.
www.theshawcenter.com

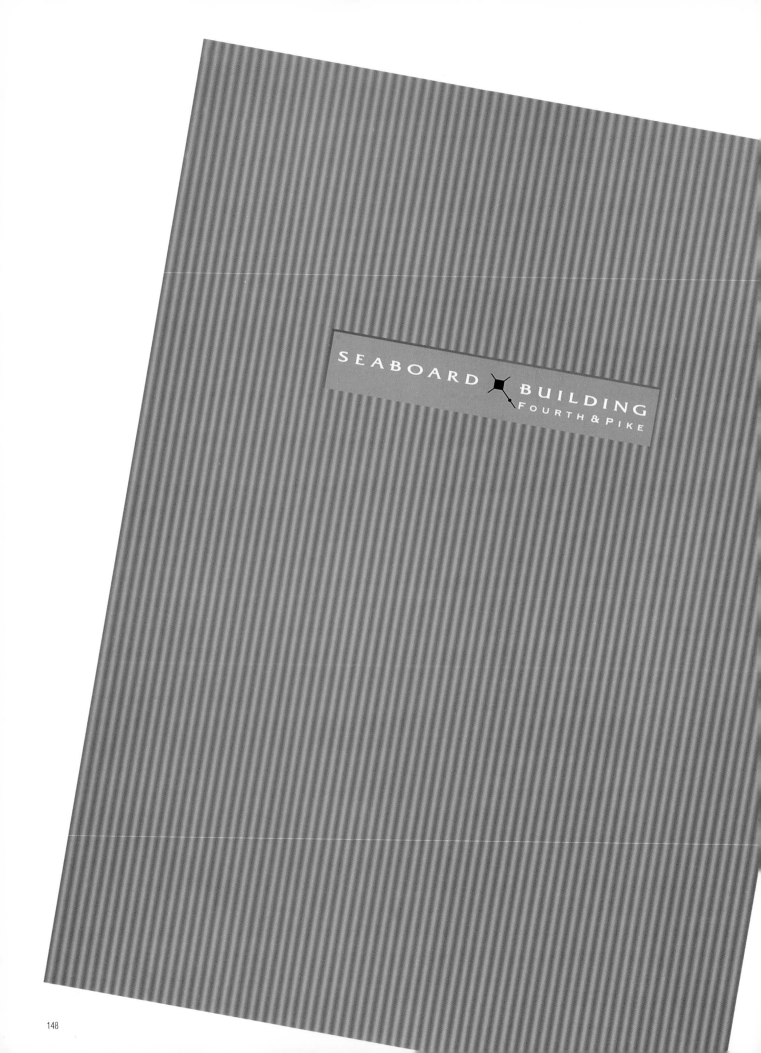

SEABOARD ✕ BUILDING
FOURTH & PIKE

Netscape: Williams Marketing: Seattle Condominium Real Estate Specialists

Back | Forward | Reload | Home | Search | Netscape | Images | Print | Security | Stop

Location: http://www.williams-marketing.com/seaboard/site_seaboard_main.htm

WebMail | People | Yellow Pages | Download | New & Cool | Network Solutio | wotch.com

WILLIAMS MARKETING, INC.
REAL ESTATE SALES & MARKETING

Print version | Seaboard Building

WMI History
Communities
• Seattle
  Northend
  Eastside
  Southend
Builder Services
Contact us

Floor Plans

Back To Top

SEABOARD BUILDING FOURTH & PIKE

Nearly one century after it was built, the Seaboard Building unites the past and future with these exquisite new one- and two-bedroom condominium homes.

The exterior of the building is a beautifully restored antique. But, within its historic brick facade, the two dozen residences are thoroughly contemporary. Homes are richly appointed and equipped with state-of-the-art appliances.

From the Seaboard Building, the city is at your door.

Now Pre-selling!

Take a virtual reality tour of two computer-generated finished homes!

Virtual Reality Tour
[Click Here!]

General Information

Address:
Fourth Avenue & Pike Street
in downtown Seattle

Site Sales Manager:
Lynn Van Lierop
Williams Marketing, Inc.

Phone:
(206) 839-0200
(206) 284-1152 (fax)
email_seaboard@uswest.net

Open Hours:
Now pre-selling. By appointment only.
Homes will be completed in early 2001.

Developer/Owner:
Pine Street Associates II L.L.C., the team that
developed Pacific Place

Price Range

1 Bedroom Starting at $450,000
2 Bedroom Starting at $685,000
2 Bedroom + Den Starting at $765,000

Features

● Beautifully restored landmark building
● Over-sized windows that open
● Durable, sound-absorbing concrete construction
● Two dozen exquisitely appointed condominium homes
● "Great room" concept with large living, dining and kitchen areas
● Hardwood floors in kitchen, living and dining areas
● Richly appointed kitchens with granite countertops and state-of-the-art appliances, including Viking gas ranges, Sub-Zero refrigerators, and Miele dishwashers
● Technologically advanced communications
● Controlled-access lobby entry and elevators
● Lobby concierge
● Rooftop deck
● The building's landmark status ensures reduced fixed real estate property taxes for ten years

Directions

The Seaboard Building is at the northeast corner of the intersection of Fourth Avenue and Pike Street.

From Interstate 5 northbound, take the Seneca Street exit; continue west on Seneca to Fourth Avenue; turn right on Fourth Avenue and continue three blocks to Pike Street.

From Interstate 5 southbound, take the Union Street exit; continue west on Union to Fourth Avenue; turn right on Fourth Avenue and continue one block to Pike Street.

SEABOARD BUILDING FOURTH & PIKE

EQUAL HOUSING OPPORTUNITY

WILLIAMS MARKETING, INC.
REAL ESTATE SALES & MARKETING

In the interest of continuing product improvement, the Seller reserves the right to make modifications to the product design, pricing and specifications without notice. Suite sizes are as per the survey. Final floor plans and square footages may vary.
PRICES ARE SUBJECT TO CHANGE WITHOUT NOTICE.

Client
Seaboard Building
Design Firm
Hornall Anderson Design Works, Inc.
Seattle, Washington
Designers
Katha Dalton, Tobi Brown,
Tiffany Scheiblauer, Ed Lee

149

SEABOARD
BUILDING
FOURTH & PIKE

Williams Marketing, Inc.
2264 15th Avenue West
Seattle, Washington 98119
www.seaboardbuilding.com

THE CITY AT YOUR DOOR

Client
Seaboard Building
Design Firm
**Hornall Anderson
Design Works, Inc.**
(continued)

SEABOARD ▮ BUILDING
FOURTH & PIKE

www.seaboardbuilding.com

Williams Marketing, Inc.
2264 15th Avenue West
Seattle, Washington 98119
www.seaboardbuilding.com

SEABOARD ▮ BUILDING
FOURTH & PIKE

Evelyne Rozner
Condo Test Case

The Rozner Company
1500 Fourth Avenue, Suite 1100
Seattle, Washington 98101
p: 206.689.0466   *f:* 206.622.6541
e: erozner@lcl.com

Client
Blue Nile
Design Firm
Hornall Anderson Design Works, Inc.
Seattle, Washington
Designers
Jack Anderson, Bruce Stigler,
Gretchen Cook, Henry Yiu,
Andrew Smith

blue nile

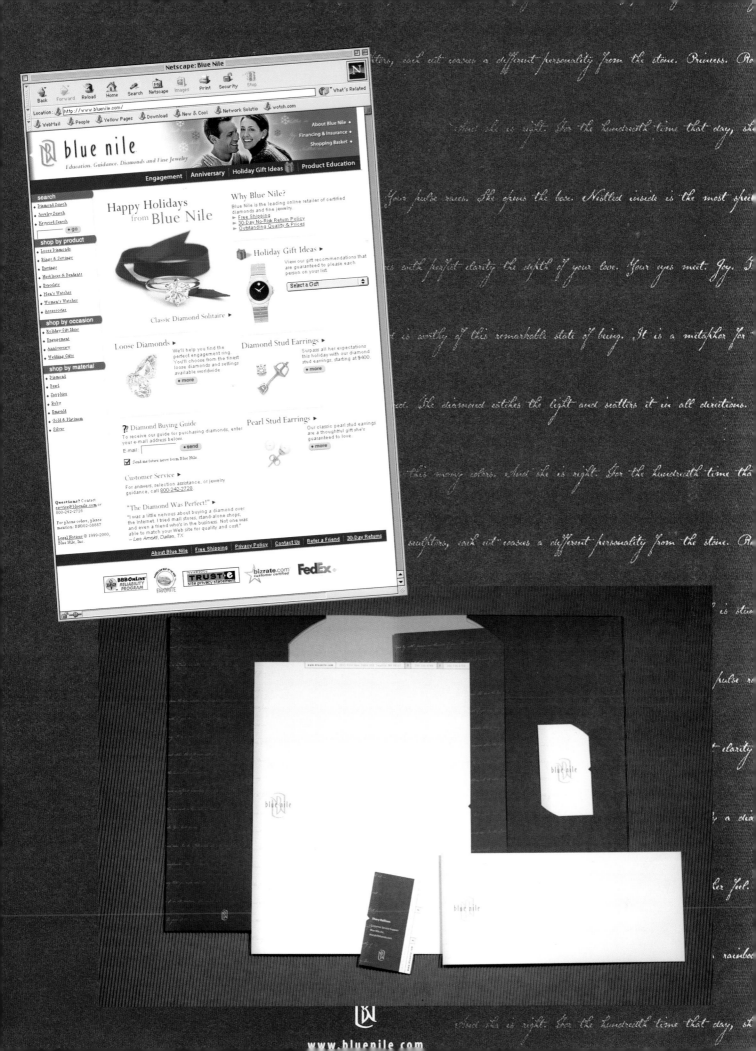

STRAY DOG

STRaY Dog RUSH CARD

PRE-PAID

STRAY DOG 17530 VASHON HWY SW VASHON, WA 98070

Client
Stray Dog Cafe
Design Firm
The Traver Company
now Methodologie, Inc.
Seattle, Washington
Designer
Christopher Downs

STRaY Dog

...HINGTON   COFFEE ★ DINING ★ SPIRITS

VASHON ISLAND, WASHINGTON   COFFEE ★ DINING ★ SPIRITS

STRaY Dog

COFF...

17530 VASHON HWY SW
VASHON, WA 98070

T. 206 463 7833   F. 206 463 7834

WWW.THESTRAYDOGCAFE.COM

Client
Buena Vista College
"presidential letterhead"
Design Firm
Sayles Graphic Design
Des Moines, Iowa
Art Director, Designer, Illustrator
John Sayles

Ferguson, Wellman, Rudd, Purdy & Van Winkle, Inc.

Est. 1975

Registered Investment Advisors

H. Joseph Ferguson
Robin L. Freeman
Steven J. Holwerda
Mark J. Kralj
L. Wayne Purdy
James H. Rudd
Roger W. Van Winkle
Norbert J. Wellman

Ferguson, Wellman, Rudd, Purdy & Van Winkle, Inc.

Registered Investment Advisors

, Suite 1919 • Portland, Oregon 97204 • 503/226-1444 • FAX 503/226-3647

Ferguson, Wellman, Rudd, Purdy & Van Winkle, Inc.

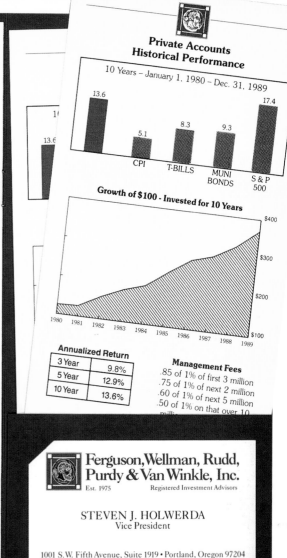

Private Accounts
Historical Performance

10 Years – January 1, 1980 – Dec. 31, 1989

13.6			17.4
	5.1	8.3	9.3
	CPI	T-BILLS	MUNI BONDS	S & P 500

Growth of $100 - Invested for 10 Years

$400
$300
$200
$100

1980 1981 1982 1983 1984 1985 1986 1987 1988 1989

Annualized Return

3 Year	9.8%
5 Year	12.9%
10 Year	13.6%

Management Fees
.85 of 1% of first 3 million
.75 of 1% of next 2 million
.60 of 1% of next 5 million
.50 of 1% on that over 10
milli...

Ferguson, Wellman, Rudd,
Purdy & Van Winkle, Inc.

Est. 1975   Registered Investment Advisors

1001 S.W. Fifth Avenue, Suite 1919 • Portland, Oregon 97204
503/226-1444   FAX 503/226-3647

Our Symbol

In ancient Greece, coins were engraved with the visage of honored gods.

Our logo features a representation of one such coin, showing the god, Dionysus. According to legend, it was Dionysus who blessed King Midas with the golden touch.

Ferguson, Wellman, Rudd,
Purdy & Van Winkle, Inc.

Est. 1975   Registered Investment Advisors

STEVEN J. HOLWERDA
Vice President

1001 S.W. Fifth Avenue, Suite 1919 • Portland, Oregon 97204
503/226-1444   FAX 503/226-3647

Client
  **Ferguson, Wellman, Rudd,
  Purdy & Van Winkle, Inc.**
Design Firm
  **Jeff Fisher LogoMotives
  Portland, Oregon**
Creative Director
  Karen Whitman
Project Coordinator
  Brenda Jacobs
Designer
  Jeff Fisher

Ferguson, Wellman, Rudd,
Purdy & Van Winkle, Inc.
Est. 1975   Registered Investment Advisors

1001 S.W. Fifth Avenue, Suite 1919 • Portland, Oregon 97204 • 503/226-1444 • FAX 503/226-3647

Ultimate Taste Experience
Fresh new look. Same great flavor.

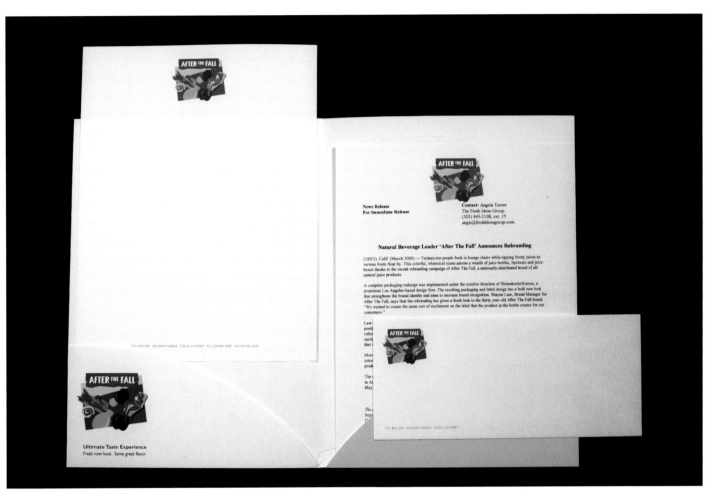

Client
Smuckers Quality Beverages
Design Firm
Shimokochi/Reeves
Los Angeles, California
Designers
Mamoru Shimokochi,
Anne Reeves

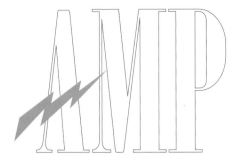

Client
AMP/Anne-Marie Petrie
Design Firm
Jeff Fisher LogoMotives
Portland, Oregon
Creative Director
Sara Perrin
Designer
Jeff Fisher

Anne-Marie Petrie
President

7575 Shelborne Drive
Granite Bay, CA 95746-8618

Phone: **916/ 797-0171**
Fax: 916/ 797-0332
E-mail: ampetrie@aol.com

Anne-Marie Petrie
7575 Shelborne Drive
Granite Bay, CA 95746-8618

7575 Shelborne Drive • Granite Bay, CA 95746-8618 • Phone: 916/ 797-0171 • Fax: 916/ 797-0332 • E-mail: ampetrie@aol.com

Client
Intermountain/RKH
Design Firm
Pollman Marketing Arts, Inc.
Boulder, Colorado
Designer
Jennifer Pollman

CHARLES A. RUSSELL

216 16th Street, Suite 770
Denver, Colorado 80202
TELEPHONE: 303 · 534 · 5409
FAX: 303 · 534 · 3322
crussell@InterMountainRKH.com
www.InterMountainRKH.com

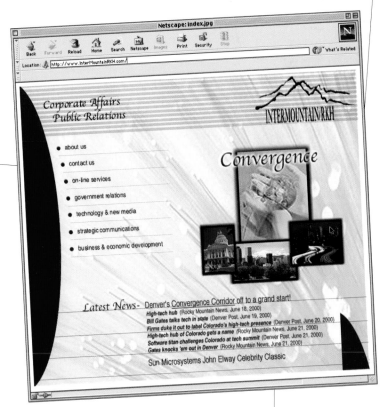

InterMountain/RKH · 216 16th Street, Suite 770 · Denver, Colorado 80202 · TELEPHONE: 303 · 534 · 5409 · FAX: 303 · 534 · 3322 · WEB: www.InterMountainRKH.com

Quantum Leaps,
No Bounds.

Littlefield
UNLIMITED
SPECIALTY MARKETING

1247 Highland Terrace
St. Louis, Missouri 63117
(314) 647-9050   Fax (314) 647-4099
www.littlefieldunlimited.com

Quantum Leaps,
No Bounds.

Littlefield
UNLIMITED
SPECIALTY·MARKETING

1247 Highland Terrace
St. Louis, Missouri 63117

It seems
they're
always
raising
the bar.

Quantum Leaps,
No Bounds.

Littlefield
UNLIMITED
SPECIALTY·MARKETING

1247 Highland Terrace
St. Louis, Missouri 63117
(314) 647-9050 • Fax (314) 647-4099
E-mail doug@littlefieldunlimited.com
www.littlefieldunlimited.com

Douglas A. Littlefield

Quantum Leaps,
No Bounds.

Littlefield
UNLIMITED
SPECIALTY·MARKETING

Fax

To _____

Fax # _____

From _____

Number of Pages _____

Message _____

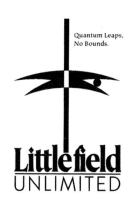

Quantum Leaps,
No Bounds.

Littlefield
UNLIMITED

When you're looking for ideas

) 647-9050 • Fax (314) 647-4099

Client
Littlefield Unlimited Specialty Marketing
Design Firm
Whitney Stinger, Inc./St. Louis
St. Louis, Missouri
Designer
Mr. Mike Whitney

PATTON BOGGS LLP
ATTORNEYS AT LAW

Client
Patton Boggs LLP
Design Firm
Greenfield/Belser Ltd.
Washington, D.C.
Designers
Burkey Belser, Marty Itner

PATTON BOGGS LLP
ATTORNEYS AT LAW
2550 M Street, NW
Washington, DC 20037-1350

Client
American Marketing Association
Design Firm
Sayles Graphic Design
Des Moines, Iowa
Art Director, Designer, Illustrator
John Sayles

IOWA
CHAPTER

AMERICAN
MARKETING
ASSOCIATION

IOWA
CHAPTER

AMERICAN
MARKETING
ASSOCIATION

P.O. BOX
7367
DES MOINES
IOWA
50509

AMERICAN
MARKETING
ASSOCIATION

EMPLOYMENT LINK

6290 Lookout Road • Boulder, CO 8030

EMPLOYMENT LINK

SENIOR
OPPORTUNITY
SOURCE

EMPLOYMENT LINK

702 10th Avenue
Longmont, CO 80501
PHONE (303) 776-4380 • FAX (303) 485-6216
WEBSITE: bcn.boulder.co.us/human-social/employmentlink

6290 Lookout Road • Boulder, CO 80301 • PHONE (303) 527-0627 • FAX (303) 527-0628 • WEBSITE bcn.boulder.co.us/human-social/employmentlink

EMPLOYMENT LINK

Client
Employment Link
Design Firm
Pollman Marketing Arts, Inc.
Boulder, Colorado
Designer
Jennifer Pollman

Client
Imind Corporation
Design Firm
Hornall Anderson Design Works, Inc.
Seattle, Washington
Designers
Jack Anderson, Debra McCloskey,
Anne Johnston, Tobi Brown,
Henry Yiu, John Anderle

imind™

education systems

A FLEISHMAN-HILLARD COMPANY

A FLEISHMAN-HILLARD COMPANY

KVO PUBLIC RELATIONS
200 SW Market Street, Suite 1400, Portland Oregon 97201-5741 / Tel 503-221-1551 Fax 503-221-0564
444 Castro Street, Suite 800, Mountain View California 94041 / Tel 650-961-1551 Fax 650-961-2728

Client
KVO Public Relations
Design Firm
Grey Matter Design
St. Louis, Missouri
Designer
Greg Maffei

ERIKA SIMMS
ACCOUNT SUPERVISOR

KVO PUBLIC RELATIONS
200 SW Market Street, Suite 1400
Portland Oregon 97201

Direct: Voice 503-221-7411 Fax 503-221-0564
erika_simms@kvo.com

Tel 503-221-1551 Fax 503-221-0564
www.kvo.com

KVO PUBLIC RELATIONS
200 SW Market Street, Suite 1400, Portland Oregon 97201-5741
Tel 503-221-1551 Fax 503-221-0564

Oregon 97201-5741

e pods

Client
epods
Design Firm
Hornall Anderson Design Works, Inc.
Seattle, Washington
Designers
Jack Anderson, Katha Dalton,
Gretchen Cook, Alan Florsheim,
Andrew Smith, Ed Lee

Netscape: ePods

Back Forward Reload Home Search Netscape Images Print Security Stop

Netsite: http://www.epods.com/

WebMail People Yellow Pages Download New & Cool Network Solutio woto

Sneak a peek at the ePods experience

e pods™   About Us   About ePodsOne™   Order Now!

$199
plus monthly
service
plans*

Introducing the ePodsOne™
Plug it in. Turn it on. ePods™ connects you to the Internet.

*Service payment plans start at $24.99 for 36 months. Upfront, 12-, 24- and 36-month payment plans are available. All plans include Internet service, a customizable page of Internet information, email, shopping, and customer support. Complete details in order process.

e pods

ePods, Inc.
2601 Fourth Ave. #400
Seattle, WA 98121
tel 206 728 9700
fax 206 728 7125

www•epods•com

www•epods•com

e pods

ePods, Inc.
2601 Fourth Ave. #400
Seattle, WA 98121

www•epods•com

www•epods•com

e pods

Anne S. Walker
Vice President, Marketing Alliance

ePods, Inc.
2601 Fourth Ave. #400
Seattle, WA 98121

tel 206 728 9700
dir 206 902 4121
fax 206 728 7125
email awalker@epods.com

www•epods•com

380 san anselmo avenue
san anselmo, california 94960

380 san anselmo avenue
san anselmo, california 94960
tele 415-256-9229
fax 415-256-9728

Client
Princess Peahead.com
Design Firm
One of One/Imagearts
Tiburon, California
Designer
Patricia Shrimpton

Suzanne Auzin

380 san anselmo avenue
san anselmo, california 94960
tele 415-256-9229
fax 415-256-9728

380 san anselmo avenue
san anselmo, california 94960
tele 415-256-9229
fax 415-256-9728

DATE: _____

P.O. # _____

SEASON: _____

S
O
L
D

T
O   Tel:

S
H
I
P

T
O   Tel:

Fax:

Start Date	Ship By	Terms	Ship Via	Special Instructions				
STYLE #	**COLOR**						Salesperson	
		DESCRIPTION						
				S	M	L	QTY.	**UNIT PRICE**	**TOTAL**

Comprehensive

Consulting

to the

Healthcare

Client
Fallbrook Engineering
Design Firm
Lorenz
San Diego, California
Designer
Arne Ratermanis

Fallbrook
Engineering

THERAPON

THERAPON

2081 dime drive

springdale, AR

72764

501-751-7345

800-443-7549

fax 501-751-8947

Client
Therapon
Design Firm
Love Packaging Group
Wichita, Kansas
Art Director
Chris West
Designer, Illustrator
Lorna West

Client
The Gifted Gardener
Design Firm
Phoenix Creative
St. Louis, Missouri
Designer
Ed Mantels-Seeker

8935 Manchester
Saint Louis, MO
63144-2621

8935 Manchester
Saint Louis, MO
63144-2621

314 / 961-1985
Fax / 961-1859

Architecture & Accessories for the Gardener

8935 Manchester
Saint Louis
Missouri 63144

Telephone: 961-1985
Area Code 314

THE GIFTED GARDENER™
Preferred Customer

C A R D H O L D E R

Please present this card to reap your rewards.
Call us at 961-1985 for fresh benefit updates.

N U M B E R .... E X P I R E S ....

Integrity

Legacy of
Positive Interaction

Humility

Client
Centegy
Design Firm
Halleck
Palo Alto, California
Designers
Wayne Wright, Daniel Tang

Centegy
Integrated e·Business Solutions

JOHN BEK
Sales Executive
john_bek@centegy.com

6539A Dumbarton Circle
Fremont, CA 94555 USA
T 510.789.1806
F 510.789.1850
M 510.468.6821

www.centegy.com

1670 S. Amphlett Blvd
Suite 214
San Mateo, CA 94402 USA

6539A Dumbarton Circle Fremont, CA 94555 USA Phone: 510.789.1820 Fax: 510.789.1850 www.centegy.com

P S O M A S

P S O M A S

P S O M A S

Client
Psomas
Design Firm
Kristin Odermatt Design
Santa Monica, California
Designers
Kristin Odermatt,
Deanna McClure

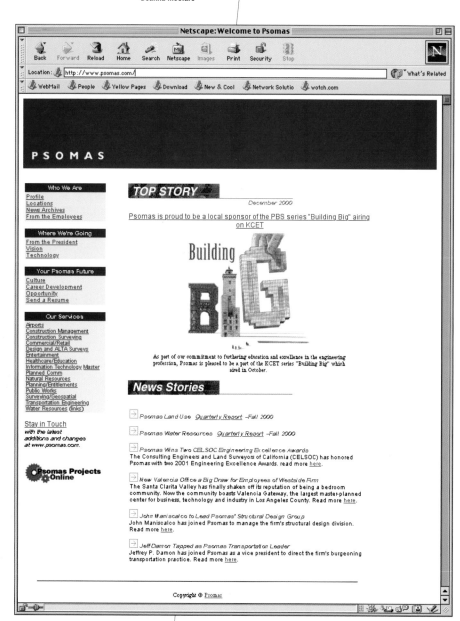

PSOMAS

Information and Engineering Solutions

PSOMAS

11444 West Olympic Blvd.
Suite 750
West Los Angeles, CA 90064-1549

PSOMAS

Timothy G. Psomas, PE
President

11444 West Olympic Blvd.
Suite 750
West Los Angeles, CA 90064

310.954.3700
310.954.3777 Fax
tpsomas@psomas.com

Information and Engineering Solutions

11444 West Olympic Blvd.
Suite 750
West Los Angeles, CA 90064-1549

310.954.3700
310.954.3777 Fax
www.psomas.com

H E A V E N L Y   S T O N E

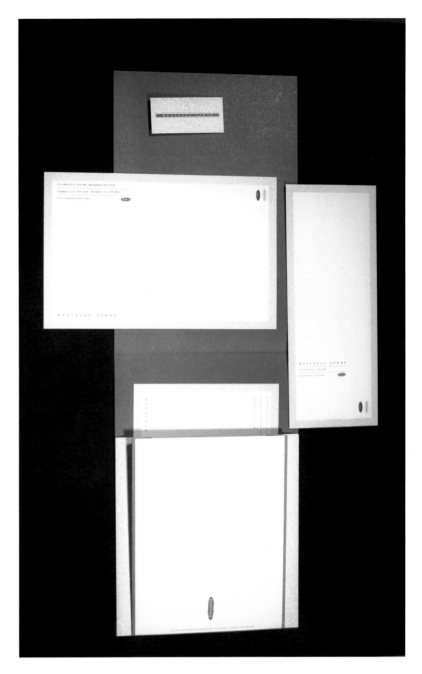

H E A V E N L Y   S T O N E

Client
Heavenly Stone
Design Firm
Hornall Anderson Design Works, Inc.
Seattle, Washington
Designers
Jack Anderson,
Henry Yiu, Taka Suzuki

ionis
INTERNATIONAL

Ionis International, Inc.
Preparing Organizations
For Success in the Pacific Rim

WorldWise, Inc. has changed its name to *Ionis International*.
Please press the "Message From Host" button below
to find out more information about this exciting change!

International Business Training Programs

- Japan Programs
- China Programs
- Pacific Region Programs
- Multicultural Team-Building Programs
- American Programs for Asians

Consulting, Interpreting, Translation, and Facilitation

- Consulting Services
- Interpreting & Translation Services
- Cultural Interpreting & Meeting Facilitation

Test Your
Knowledge

Message
From Host

For Questions and/or Comments - CONTACT US

ionis
INTERNATIONAL

ionis
INTERNATIONAL

スーザン・M・プレイス
代表取締役

ionis
INTERNATIONAL

アィオニス・インターナショナル
米国コロラド州ボルダー市
クウェイル・クリーク・レーン4725
電話 : 303-530-0680
Fax : 303-530-0305

Susan M. Place
Managing Director

4725 Quail Creek Lane
Boulder, CO 80301-3872 USA
Tel: 303 . 530 . 0680
        800 . 571 . 8831
Fax: 303 . 530 . 0305
Email: splace@ionisinternational.com

ionis
INTERNATIONAL

4725 Quail Creek Lane   Boulder, CO 80301-3872 USA
Tel: 303 . 530 . 0680   800 . 571 . 8831
Email: contact@ionisinternational.com   Fax: 303 . 530 . 0305
                                        Website: ionisinternational.com

CASSIDAY'S COLLECTIONS LLC
P.O. Box 31165, Chicago, Illinois 60631-0165
PHONE 773 774 5700   FAX 773 792 9591   E-MAIL cassidays-collections.com

BETH CASSIDAY

CASSIDAY'S COLLECTIONS
5750 N. EAST CIRCLE AVENUE, CHICAGO, ILLINOIS 60631
PHONE 773 792 9378   FAX 773 792 9591
E-MAIL bcassiday@hotmail.com

Client
Starry Night
Design Firm
JOED Design Inc.
Elmhurst, Illinois
Designer
Edward Rebek

dever designs

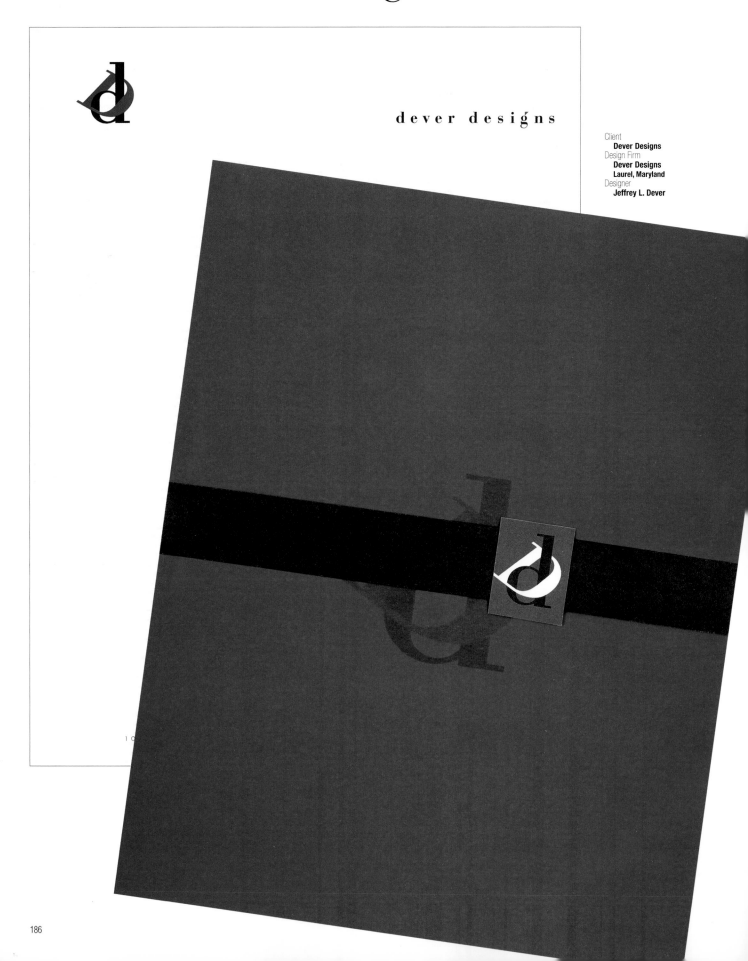

dever designs

Client
Dever Designs
Design Firm
Dever Designs
Laurel, Maryland
Designer
Jeffrey L. Dever

dever designs

dever designs 1056 WEST STREET ▪ LAUREL ▪ MARYLAND ▪ 20707-3531

dever designs

1056 WEST STREET, LAUREL, MD 20707 ▪ TEL 301-776-2812 ▪ FAX 301-953-1196

1056 WEST STREET, LAUREL, MD 20707
TEL 301-776-2812 ▪ FAX 301-953-1196

dever designs

JEFFREY L. DEVER
PRESIDENT—CREATIVE DIRECTOR

1056 WEST STREET, LAUREL, MD 20707
TEL 301-776-2812 ▪ FAX 301-953-1196

the point
where art
and
communication
meet

dever designs

JEFFREY L. DEVER
PRESIDENT—CREATIVE DIRECTOR

OLSON
SUNDBERG
KUNDIG ALLEN
A R C H I T E C T S

Client
Olson Sundberg Kundig Allen
Design Firm
Girvin, Inc.
Seattle, Washington
Designers
Rob Berreth, Tim Girvin

THE ELLIOTT

Joseph P. LaBreche
Associate Director of Sales

THE ELLIOTT

721 Pine Street
Seattle, WA 98101
t 206.262.0700
f 206.625.1221
labreche@theelliott.com
www.elliotthotel.com

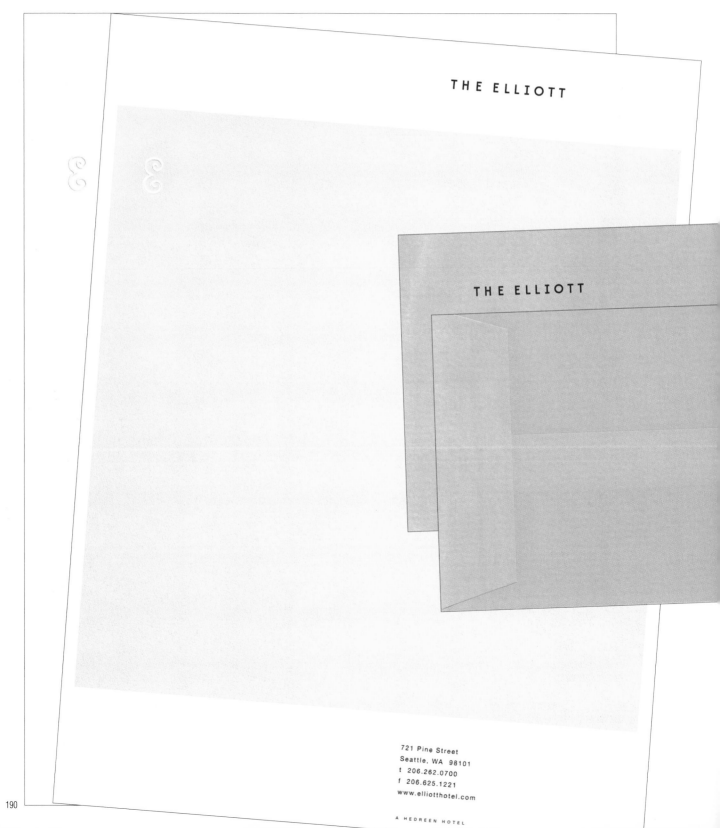

THE ELLIOTT

THE ELLIOTT

721 Pine Street
Seattle, WA 98101
t 206.262.0700
f 206.625.1221
www.elliotthotel.com

A HEDREEN HOTEL

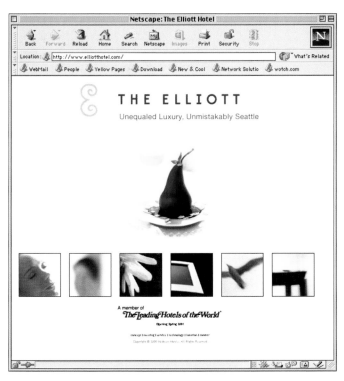

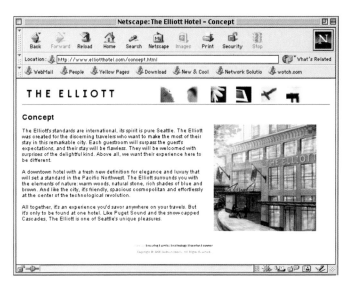

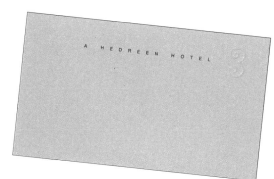

Client
**The Elliott Hotel
(R.C. Hedreen)**

Design Firm
**The Traver Company
now Methodologie, Inc.
Seattle, Washington**

Designers
**Dale Hart, Christopher Downs,
Margo Sepanski**

überfax

to ....

company ....

from ....

date .... (including this cover sheet)

fax# ....

pages ....

notes:

über

über, inc.

herta kriegner
president

231 w 29ᵗʰ st, #1204
new york, ny 10001
tel 212.643 1135
fax 212.643.1205
herta@uber-inc.com

über, inc. • 231 west 29ᵗʰ street, #1204 • new york, ny 10001
tel 212.643.1135 • fax 212.643.1205 • e-mail info@uber-inc.com

über, inc.

inc.

über, inc.

29ᵗʰ st, #1204
ork, ny 10001
2.643.1135
212.643.1205

new york, ny 10001
• fax 212.643.1205 • e-mail info@uber-inc.com

Client
über, inc.
Design Firm
über, inc.
New York, New York
Designers
Herta Kriegner,
Suzanne Jennerich

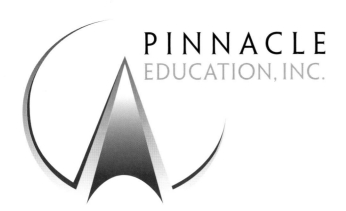

PINNACLE
EDUCATION, INC.

Client
Pinnacle Education
Design Firm
**Sullivan Marketing &
Communications
Phoenix, Arizona**
Designer
Jack Sullivan

PINNACLE
HIGH SCHOOL

TEMPE

2224 W. Southern Ave. #2
Tempe, Arizona 85282
Tel. 602.414.0950
Fax 602.414.0927

PINNACLE
HIGH SCHOOL

409 W. McMurray Blvd
Casa Grande, Arizona 85222

PINNACLE
HIGH SCHOOL

151 N. Centennial Way
Mesa, Arizona 85201

PINNACLE
HIGH SCHOOL

2224 W. Southern Ave. #2
Tempe, Arizona 85282

CAMPUS LOCATIONS: Casa Grande/Mesa/Tempe
www.pin-ed.com

PINNACLE
HIGH SCHOOL

MESA

151 N. Centennial Way
Mesa, Arizona 85201
Tel. 480.668.5003
Fax 480.668.5005

PINNACLE
HIGH SCHOOL

CASA GRANDE

409 W. McMurray Blvd.
Casa Grande, Arizona 85222
Tel. 520.423.2380
Fax 520.423.2383

CAMPUS LOCATIONS: Casa Grande/Mesa/Tempe
w w w . p i n - e d . c o m

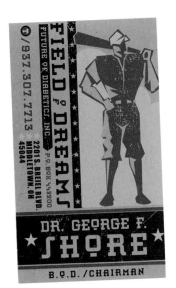

FIELD of DREAMS
FUTURE OF DIABETICS, INC.

MIDDLETOWN, OHIO

SPONSO

Thank You

FIELD of DREAMS
★ FUTURE OF DIABETICS, INC. ★

Client
Future of Diabetics, Inc.
Design Firm
Visual Marketing Associates
Dayton, Ohio
Designers
Kenneth Botts, Jason Selke

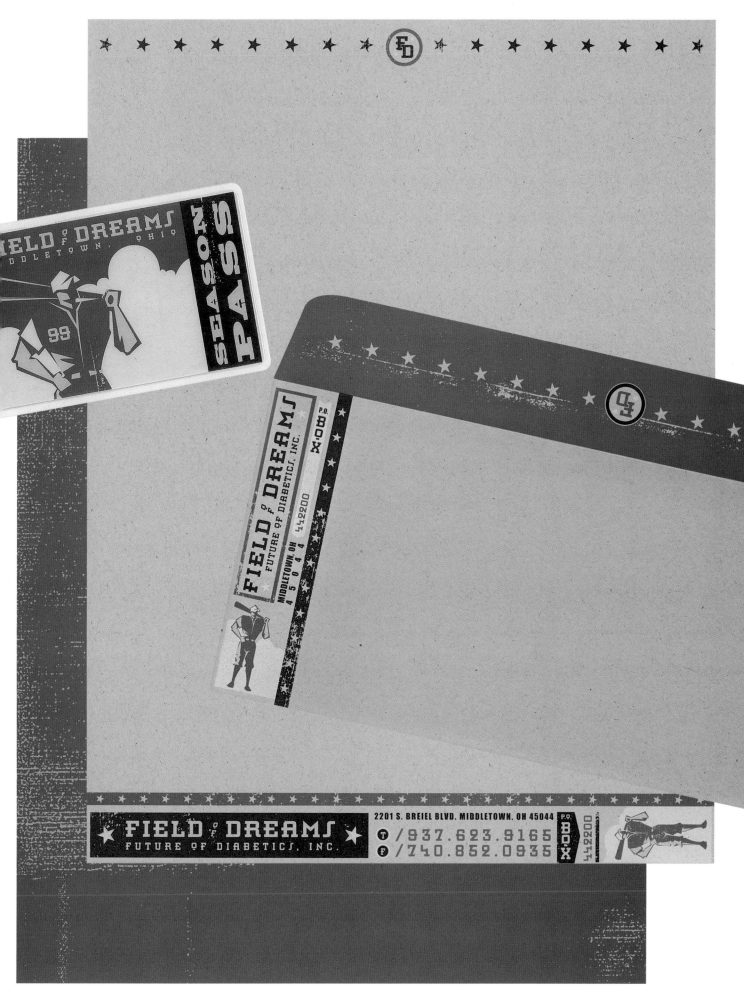

FIELD of DREAMS
FUTURE of DIABETICS, INC.

2201 S. BREIEL BLVD. MIDDLETOWN, OH 45044
T /937.623.9165
F /740.852.0935
P.O. BOX 442200

Boston Unique Events, Inc.
CATERING

Boston Unique Events, Inc.
CATERING

Boston Unique Events, Inc.
CATERING

Boston Unique Events, Inc.
CATERING

Client
Boston Unique Events
Design Firm
Studio Izbickas
Boston, Massachusetts
Designers
Edmund V. Izbickas,
Susan Callender

Boston Unique Events, Inc.
CATERING

SUSAN JOY CALLENDER

Boston Unique Events, Inc.
CATERING

39 ALLSTON STREET
BOSTON
MASSACHUSETTS 02124-2225
PH (617) 282-6000
FAX (617) 282-5209

Boston Unique Events, Inc.
CATERING
39 ALLSTON STREET, BOSTON, MASSACHUSETTS 02124-2225

Client
Mary Brandon
Design Firm
Shimokochi/Reeves
Los Angeles, California
Designers
Mamoru Shimokochi,
Anne Reeves

MARY BRANDON
Director

139 Murray Street

Darling Harbour

Pyrmont NSW 2009

Phone (02) 552 3755

Fax (02) 552 3501

139 Murray Street · Darling Harbour · Pyrmont NSW 2009

139 Murray Street · Darling Harbour · Pyrmont NSW 2009 · Phone (02) 552 3755 · Fax (02) 552 3501

THE MANSION
at MGM Grand

3799 LAS VEGAS BOULEVARD SOUTH   LAS VEGAS, NEVADA 89109

3799 LAS VEGAS BOULEVARD SOUTH   LAS VEGAS, NEVADA 89109   702.891.5888 TELEPHONE   702.891.5880 FACSIMILE

3799 LAS VEGAS BOULEVARD SOUTH   LAS VEGAS, NEVADA 89109

Client
The Mansion at MGM Grand
Design Firm
David Carter Design Assoc.
Dallas, Texas
Designer
Ashley Barron

THE MANSION
at MGM Grand

THE MANSION
at MGM Grand

THE MANSION
at MGM Grand

ALFONSO RIOS *Butler*

3799 LAS VEGAS BOULEVARD SOUTH
LAS VEGAS, NEVADA 89109
702.891.5870 TELEPHONE 702.891.5884 FACSIMILE

THE MANSION
at MGM Grand

Client
Good Times Jazz Festival
Design Firm
Sayles Graphic Design
Des Moines, Iowa
Art Director, Designer, Illustrator
John Sayles

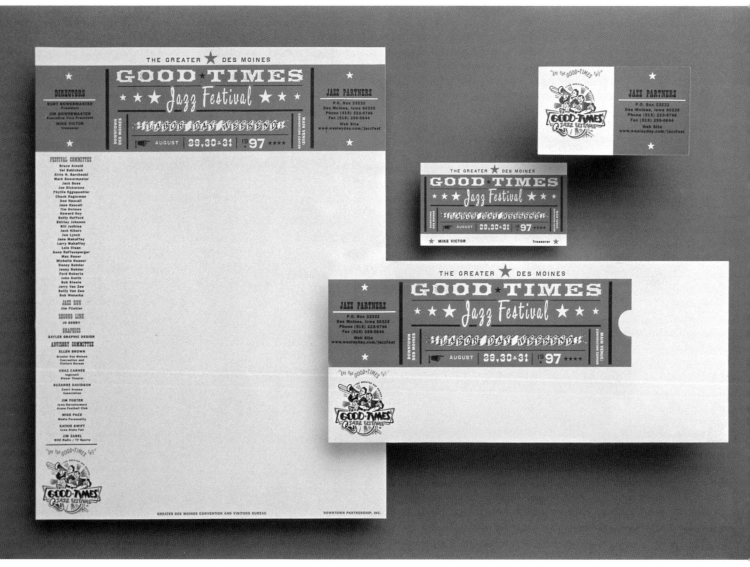

DENNIS
CREWS
PHOTOGRAPHY

Client
Dennis Crews
Design Firm
Dever Designs
Laurel, Maryland
Designer
Jeffrey L. Dever

DENNIS
CREWS
PHOTOGRAPHY

809-C
E. South
Street,
Frederick,
Maryland
21701

301-696-9123

DENNIS CREWS PHOTOGRAPHY

809-C East South St.
Frederick, MD 21701

809-C East South Street, Frederick, Maryland 21701

THE CYPRESS CENTER

THE CYPRESS CENTER

Innovative physical therapy and fitness

970 Monument Street, Suite 207
Pacific Palisades, California 90272
310.573.9553 phone / 310.573.9533 fax
cypresscenter@aol.com

THE CYPRESS CENTER

Innovative physical therapy and fitness

Name: _____   Frequency: _____ X Weekly For _____ Weeks

Date: _____ Next Appointment Date: _____   Precautions/Contraindications _____

Diagnosis: _____   Referring Physician: _____

_____   Physician's Signature: _____

PHYSICAL THERAPY PRESCRIPTION

____ **Evaluate and Treat**

____ **Evaluation**
   cervical
   thoracic cage
   lumbar
   pelvis/sacro-iliac
   upper extremity
   lower extremity
   neurological
   cardiac
   pulmonary
   postural
   other _____

____ **Manual Therapy**
   soft-tissue mobilization
   joint mobilization
   massage
   myofascial release
   dural/nerve mobilization
   manual stretching/PROM

____ **Modalities**
   moist heat
   cryotherapy
   e-stim/interferential
   ultrasound
   iontophoresis

____ **Traction**
   cervical
   lumbar
   anti-gravity

____ **Therapeutic Exercise**
   A/AAROM
   progressive resistive exercise
   Pilates method of conditioning
   Gyrotonics exercise system
   Hatha/Ashtanga yoga methods
   cardiopulmonary conditioning
   sports specific training
   home exercise program

Rehabilitation Programs
____ trunk stabilization
____ postural re-education
____ pre/post natal program
____ TMJ dysfunction
____ neurological rehabilitation

Preventative Care & Patient Education
____ chronic pain management
____ stress management
____ weight management
____ arthritis/osteoporosis

970 Monument Street, Suite 207 • Pacific Palisades, California 90272 • 310.573.9553 phone / 310.573.9533 fax • cypresscenter@aol.com

Daniella Maysels
Physical Therapist

970 Monument Street, Suite 207
Pacific Palisades, California 90272
310.573.9553 phone / 310.573.9533 fax
cypresscenter@aol.com

THE CYPRESS CENTER

Client
The Cypress Center
Design Firm
Treehouse Design
Culver City, California
Designer
Tricia Rauen

THE CYPRESS CENTER

Innovative physical therapy and fitness

970 Monument Street, Suite 207
Pacific Palisades, California 90272

Client
ROR
Design Firm
Shimokochi/Reeves
Los Angeles, California
Designers
Mamoru Shimokochi,
Anne Reeves

Managing Director/
Executive Producer

Misato Shinohara

175 E. Olive Ave., Suite 200 • Burbank, CA 91502
Phone: 818.526.4889 • Fax: 818.526.4884

175 E. Olive Ave., Suite 200 • Burbank, CA 91502

175 E. Olive Ave., Suite 200 • Burbank, CA 91502
Phone: 818.526.4889 • Fax: 818.526.4884

Client
PlanetExchange
Design Firm
Bjornson Design Associates, Inc.
Philadelphia, Pennsylvania
Designer
Jon Anders Bjornson

Client
TriAd
Design Firm
Jeff Fisher LogoMotives
Portland, Oregon
Creative Director
Sue Fisher
Designer
Jeff Fisher

1197 NW Wall • Bend, OR 97701-1934

Sue Fisher
President

541/389-4970
Fax: 541/389-1285

results@TriAd-agency.com

1197 NW Wall
Bend, Oregon 97701

1197 NW Wall • Bend, Oregon 97701-1934 • 541/389-4970 • Fax: 541/389-1285 • triad@empnet.com

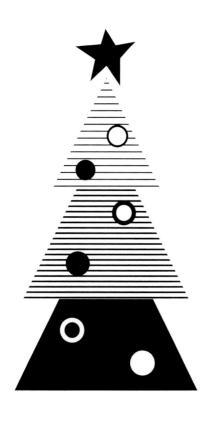

New & Improved!

TriAd
CAN DO!

Est. 1993

Great Ideas

**ADVERTISING
MARKETING
PUBLIC RELATIONS**

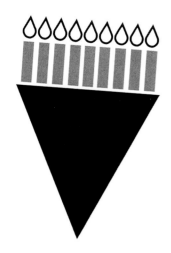

No matter how
you look at it,
our wish for you
is black and white:
Happy Holidays!

TriAd
Advertising • Marketing • Public Relations

ENVIRO-SOLUTIONS, INC.

GDC

822 NEOSHO AVENUE
BATON ROUGE, LA 70802
TEL: (504) 383-8556
FAX: (504) 383-2789

RUDY SAXTON
PROJECT DEVELOPMENT

GDC

ENVIRO-SOLUTIONS, INC.

Client
GDC Enviro-Solutions, Inc.
Design Firm
William Homan Design
Richfield, Minnesota
Designer
William Homan

N B L   T E C H N O L O G I E S ,   I N C .
AN AFFILIATE OF GDC ENVIRO-SOLUTIONS, INC.

E N V I R O - S O L U T I O N S ,   I N C .

GDC

822

NEOSHO

AVENUE

BATON

ROUGE

LOUISIANA

70802

TEL: (504)

383-8556

FAX: (504)

383-2789

NBL

TECHNOLOGIES

INC.

P.O. BOX 591

MT. PLEASANT

SOUTH

CAROLINA

29464

TEL: (803)

884-5903

FAX: (803)

849-1591

GDC

ENVIRO-

SOLUTIONS

INC.

822

NEOSHO

AVENUE

BATON

ROUGE

LOUISIANA

70802

TEL: (504)

383-8566

FAX: (504)

383-2789

NBL TECHNOLOGIES, INC.

AN AFFILIATE OF GDC ENVIRO-SOLUTIONS, INC.

GDC

ENVIRO-SOLUTIONS, INC.

NBL
TECHNOLOGIES
INC.
P.O. BOX 591
MT. PLEASANT
SOUTH
CAROLINA
29464
TEL: (803)
884-5903
FAX: (803)
849-1591

GDC
ENVIRO-
SOLUTIONS
INC.

GDC ENVIRO-S

Client
GDC Enviro-Solutions, Inc.
Design Firm
William Homan Design
(continued)

E N V I R O - S O L U T I O N S ,   I N C .

GDC

822

NEOSHO

AVENUE

BATON

ROUGE

LOUISIANA

70802

TEL: (504)

GDC

E N V I R O - S O L U T I O N S ,

B 2 2
N E O S H O
A V E N U E
B A T O N
R O U G E
L O U I S I A N A
7 0 8 0 2

E N V I R O - S O L U T I O N S ,   I N C .

GDC

822 NEOSHO AVENUE
BATON ROUGE, LA 70802
TEL: (504) 383-8556
FAX: (504) 383-2789

JAN BERKOWITZ
PRESIDENT, NBL TECHNOLOGIES, INC.

L   U   T   I   O   N   S ,   I   N   C .

Shop Local.com

Client
Shoplocal.com
Design Firm
Girvin, Inc.
Seattle, Washington
Designers
Jeff Lancaster, Rob Berreth

311 ½ Occidental Ave S. Suite 300
Seattle, Washington 98104

Shop Local.com
311 ½ Occidental Ave S. Suite 300
Seattle, Washington 98104

MYRIO™

Leveraging your Lines.

Myrio Corporation
3500 Carillon Point
Kirkland, WA 98033

MYRIO™

Myrio Corporation
3500 Carillon Point
Kirkland, WA 98033

tel 425 897 7200   www.myrio.com
fax 425 897 5600

Mark Rowe
Vice President, Finance

Myrio Corporation
3500 Carillon Point
Kirkland, WA 98033

tel 425 897 7215
fax 425 897 5600
cell 425 234 4680

mark.rowe@myrio.com

MYRIO™

MYRIO™

Leveraging your Lines.

Please deliver the following pages to:

Date of transmission:

Total number of pages:

Company:

Tel:

Transmission is from:

Fax:

Regarding:

e-mail address:

⭕ Urgent   ⭕ For Review   ⭕ Please Comment   ⭕ Please Reply

Comments:

If this transmission is incomplete, please notify us at once.

Myrio Corporation
3500 Carillon Point
Kirkland, WA 98033

tel 425 897 7200
fax 425 897 5600

www.myrio.com

Client
MYRIO
Design Firm
Girvin, Inc.
Seattle, Washington
Designers
Rob Berreth

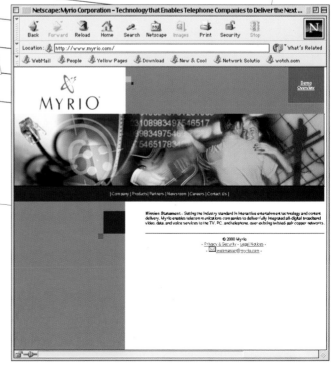

PORTICO
CHERRY CREEK

DENVER COLORADO 80206
155-B FILLMORE STREET

CHERRY CREEK

155-B FILLMORE STREET
DENVER COLORADO 80206
303.758.7611 FAX 303.377.4733

CHERRY CREEK

FILLMORE

ER COLORADO 80206

La Dolce Vita

PORTICO
CHERRY CREEK

Client
Kestrel Partners/Portico
Design Firm
Ellen Bruss Design
Denver, Colorado
Designers
Ellen Bruss, Charles Carpenter

PORTICO
CHERRY CREEK

DAWN RAYMOND

BROKER ASSOCIATE

155-B FILLMORE STREET
DENVER COLORADO 80206
303.758.7611 FAX 303.377.4733
V-MAIL 303.758.5888 EXT 275
MOBILE 303.777.7177

Join us at our sales office

155-B Fillmore Denver, Colorado
303.758.7611

Prime Location Steps Away From Cherry Creek Bike Path,

Shopping Center, Restaurants and Galleries. Unparalleled Amenities, Including

Year Round Heated Pool & Jacuzzi, Sundeck, Fitness Center, State-of-the-Art

Security & Underground Parking. Luxury Finishes Featuring Gas Fireplaces,

Granite Slab Counters, Hardwood Floors & Private Terraces.

Floor Plans Ranging from 900 to Almost 4,000 Square Feet.

Priced from $200,000 to Over 1.5 Million.

PORTICO
CHERRY CREEK

Client
Beverly Sassoon International
Design Firm
Shimokochi/Reeves
Los Angeles, California
Designers
Mamoru Shimokochi,
Anne Reeves

Beverly Sassoon International, LLC

501 Brickell Key Drive

Suite 505

Miami, Florida 33131

Tel: (305) 358-0031

Fax: (305) 358-8202

www.bsassoon.com

Beverly Sassoon
Chairman

Beverly Sassoon International, LLC
501 Brickell Key Drive, Suite 505
Miami, Florida 33131
Tel: (305) 358-0031
Fax: (305) 358-8202
e-mail: beverly@bsassoon.com

Beverly Sassoon International, LLC

501 Brickell Key Drive, Suite 505

Miami, Florida 33131

IMPROVISATIONAL
LEARNING SYSTEMS

IMPROVISATIONAL
LEARNING SYSTEMS

106 Corporate Park Drive   Suite 101, White Plains, NY 10604

106 Corporate Park Drive
Suite 101, White Plains, NY 10604
T 914 251 1336 **F** 914 251 1335
toll free 877 772 7962
W ils-team.com

Client
  Improvisational Learning Systems
Design Firm
  McDill Design
  Milwaukee, Wisconsin
Designers
  Brad Bedessem, Michael Dillon

CORPORATE TRAINING
AT THE SPEED OF LAUGH

ceiling

Flos USA Mono ceiling fixture, with glass diffuser
for downlight and a reflector for a radial starburst
design. colors: glass white enamel. designer:
Achille Castiglioni. lamps: 1 x 100 watt halogen

suspension

< >

Flos USA Aurora glass suspension fixture
providing downlight and ambient light. colors:
dark blue, anthracite gray. designer: P.A. King, S.
Miranda. lamps: 1 x 50 watt. halogen.

contact us

Roy Anthony Laciura
President

Client
Lightmakers
Design Firm
Courage Design
Buffalo, New York
Designer
Alan Kegler

Lightmakers of NY

125 Elmwood Ave.

Buffalo, NY

14201

Roy Anthony Laciura
President

Lightmakers of NY

125 Elmwood Ave.

Buffalo, NY

14201

716 885 4448 phone

716 885 6940 fax

www.light-makers.com

Lightmakers of NY

125 Elmwood Ave.

Buffalo, NY

14201

716 885 4448 phone

716 885 6940 fax

Client
Goodwin Tucker Group
Design Firm
Sayles Graphic Design
Des Moines, Iowa
Art Director, Designer, Illustrator
John Sayles

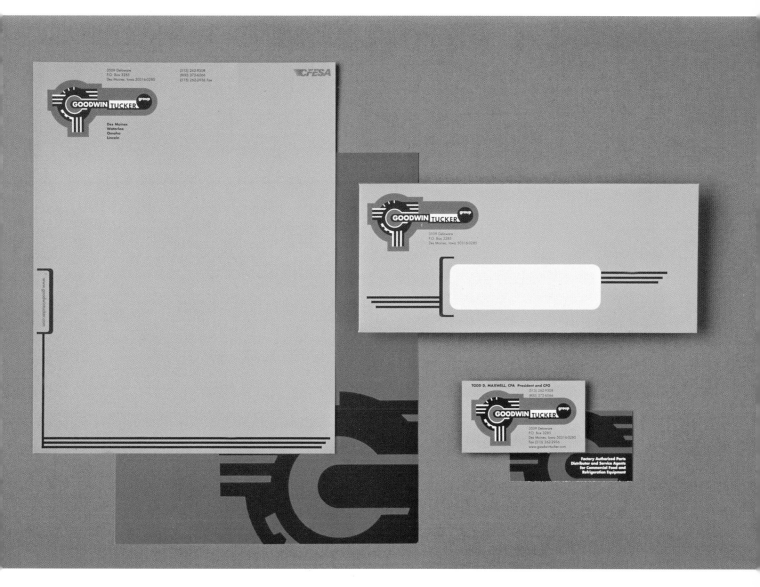

Client
Merchandising East
Design Firm
Axis Communications
Washington, D.C.
Designer
Charlyne Fabi

MERCHANDISING EAST
Interior Architecture & Design

555 Main Street, Laurel, Maryland 20707
TEL 301 490 7700 FAX 301 498 6634
merchandisingeast.com

MERCHANDISING

In

 MERCHANDISI Main Street, Laurel, Maryland 20707
Int... TEL 301 490 7700 FAX 301 498 6634
merchandisingeast.com

 MERCHANDISING
Interior A

 MERCHANDISING EAST
Interior Architecture & Design

555 Main Street, Laurel, Maryland 20707
TEL 301 490 7700 FAX 301 498 6634

Melissa Florschutz, *Interior Designer*

Client
Rutherford Investment Management
Design Firm
Jeff Fisher LogoMotives
Portland, Oregon

Creative Director
Denny Shleifer
Designer
Jeff Fisher

William D. Rutherford

6978 SW Foxfield Court
Suite 200
Portland, OR 97225

Phone: 503/ 291-1140 • Fax: 503/ 291-1138
Cellular: 503/ 701-8547 • wrutherford@msn.com

6978 SW Foxfield Court
Suite 200
Portland, OR 97225

6978 SW Foxfield Court
Suite 200
Portland, OR 97225

Phone: 503/ 291-1140 • Fax: 503/ 291-1138 • Cellular: 503/ 701-8547 • wrutherford@msn.com

Client
**Rutherford
Investment
Management**
Design Firm
**Jeff Fisher
LogoMotives**
(continued)

6978 SW Foxfield Court
Suite 200
Portland, OR 97225

6978 SW Foxfield Court
Suite 200
Portland, OR 97225

William D. Rutherford

6978 SW Foxfield Court
Suite 200
Portland, OR 97225

Phone: 503/ 291-1140 • Fax: 503/ 291-1138
Cellular: 503/ 701-8547 • wrutherford@msn.com

Chava LeBarton
Executive Vice President
of Curriculum and Co-Founder

chava@xow.com

8695
West
Washington
Boulevard

Suite 201

Culver City
California
90232

Phone
310-558-9000
Fax
310-815-9489

www.xow.com

Client
XOW!
Design Firm
Hornall Anderson Design Works, Inc.
Seattle, Washington
Designers
Jack Anderson, Lisa Cerveny,
Bruce Branson-Meyer, Don Stayner,
Mary Chin Hutchison

8695
West
Washington
Boulevard

Suite 201

Culver City
California
90232

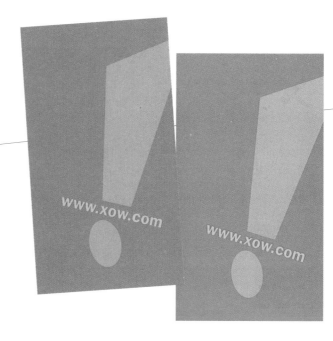

www.xow.com

www.xow.com

8695
West
Washington
Boulevard

Suite 201

Culver City
California
90232

8695
West
Washington
Boulevard

Suite 201

Culver City
California
90232

www.xow.com

www.XOW.com

Phone
310-558-9000

Fax
310-815-9489

Client
Eventra
Design Firm
Tom Fowler, Inc.
Norwalk, Connecticut
Designer
Karl S. Maruyama

eventra

Shaping EC solutions for the
direct material supply chain™

eventra

Shaping EC solutions for the
direct material supply chain™

Merritt Crossing
440 Wheelers Farms Road
Milford, Connecticut 06460

T 203.882.9988
F 203.882.9946
W www.eventra.com

Merritt Crossing
440 Wheelers Farms Road
Milford, Connecticut 06460

eventra

Shaping EC solutions for the
direct material supply chain™

A new name for the APL Group, Inc.

Qualedi Software
Web Applications
Professional Services

Pat Stites
Marketing Director

eventra

Shaping EC solutions for the
direct material supply chain™

Merritt Crossing
440 Wheelers Farms Road
Milford, Connecticut 06460

T 877.EVENTRA (383.6872)
F 203.882.9946
EM pstites@eventra.com
W www.eventra.com

A new name for the APL Group, Inc.

eventra

Shaping EC solutions for the
direct material supply chain™

Merritt Crossing
440 Wheelers Farms Road
Milford, Connecticut 06460

A new name for the APL Group, Inc.

Qualedi® Software | Web Applications | Professional Services

eventra

Shaping EC solutions for
the heart of...

eventra

Shaping EC solutions for
the heart of your...

eventra

Shaping EC solutions for
the heart of your business™

A new name for the APL Group, Inc.

Web Applications

Qualedi Software

Professional Services

eventra

HEADLINE NEWS

SHAPING EC SOLUTIONS FOR THE DIRECT MATERIAL SUPPLY CHAIN™

company

supply chain
solutions

management team
partners
career opportunities
locations
information request

consulting
services

news/events

contact us

Overview

Eventra leads the way in supply chain solutions configured for
collaboration between manufacturers and their direct material
suppliers. Our VendorSite customers are leading companies who seek
dramatic improvements in supply chain efficiency and reduced costs
associated with product parts planning.

Eventra is wholly focused on providing the solutions and services
needed to manage the inbound supply chain successfully. First to
market with a solution for direct material procurement, VendorSite
delivers comprehensive capabilities that provide a complete window
into the inbound supply chain.

To find out more about Eventra, click on one of the links below.

management team

career opportunities

partners

locations

© eventra 2000 | home | company | supply chain solutions | consulting | news/events | contact us | contact web master | legal

235

™

Client
Consolidated Correctional Food Services
Design Firm
Sayles Graphic Design
Des Moines, Iowa
Art Director, Designer, Illustrator
John Sayles

 **CONSULTING ENGINEERS**

Client
ESM Consulting Engineers
Design Firm
The Traver Company
now Methodologie, Inc.
Seattle, Washington
Designers
Dale Hart, Christopher Downs

SERVICE AREAS

Civil Engineering
Land Surveying
Project Management
Public Works
Land Planning
Landscape Design

Yvette Tinsley
Marketing Manager

yvettet@esmcivil.com   Fax (253) 838 7104
Federal Way (253) 838 6113   Cell (253) 405-0866
Tacoma (253) 927 0619   720 South 348th Street
Seattle (206) 623 5911   Federal Way, WA 98003

ESM CONSULTING ENGINEERS LLC
720 South 348th Street Federal Way, WA 98003

Civil Engineering   Land Planning
Project Management   Public Works
Land Surveying

720 South 348th Street   Tel (253) 838 6113   Tacoma (253) 927 0619
Federal Way, WA 98003   Fax (253) 838 7104   Seattle (206) 623 5911
                          www.esmcivil.com   Bremerton (360) 792 3375

WINTER

appetizers

Multi-layered terrine of house-smoked Atlantic salmon and fresh
Laura Chenel goat cheese, braised baby leeks, Osetra caviar, and sal
drizzled with fresh dill vinaigrette. $11.—

Crispy crab roll with Asian spices, pe
and watercress

Poached pear and Stilton with Mizun.
and crushed black pep

Shrimp tart with parisienne vegetable

Seasoned salad of mixed gre
tossed witi

Salad of duck confit, haricot v
with curly endive, drizzled with
Asian s.

Rich bouillon of seasonal wild mus
aged Oloroso sherry, seasoned

Terrine of foie gras with sauterne gel

Selec

16 Fairgrounds Road
Hamilton, New Jersey 08619
609.584.7800

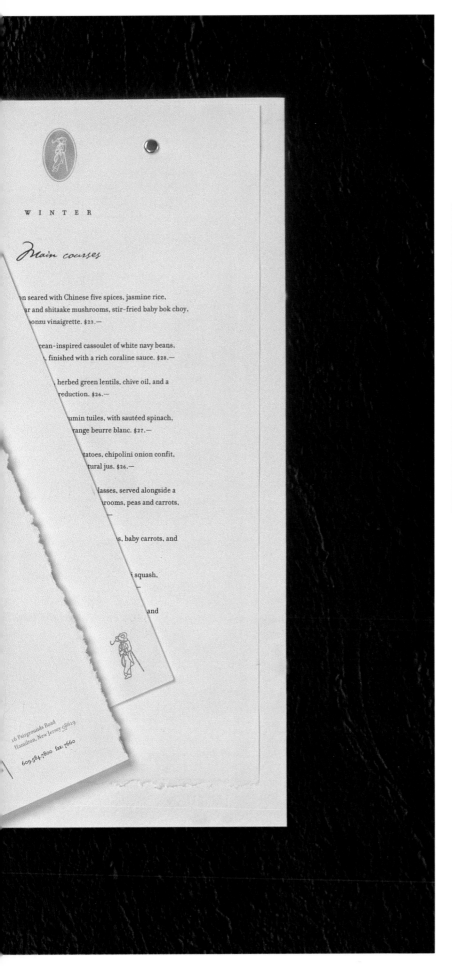

WINTER

Main courses

n seared with Chinese five spices, jasmine rice,
r and shitaake mushrooms, stir-fried baby bok choy,
onzu vinaigrette. $23.—

cean-inspired cassoulet of white navy beans,
, finished with a rich coraline sauce. $28.—

herbed green lentils, chive oil, and a
reduction. $26.—

umin tuiles, with sautéed spinach,
range beurre blanc. $27.—

tatoes, chipolini onion confit,
tural jus. $26.—

lasses, served alongside a
rooms, peas and carrots,

s, baby carrots, and

squash,

and

16 Fairgrounds Road
Hamilton, New Jersey 08619
609.584.7800 fax: 7660

J. SEWARD JOHNSON, JR.
THE BIG CHEESE

P. O. Box 550
Princeton, NJ 08542

Telephone: 609.924.6132
Fax: 609.683.7904

Client
Rats
Design Firm
Bjornson Design Associates, Inc.
Philadelphia, Pennsylvania
Designer
Jon Anders Bjornson

Seattle
Seahawks

Seattle
Seahawks

Client
 Seattle Seahawks
Design Firm
 Jeff Fisher LogoMotives
 Portland, Oregon
Creative Director
 Sara Perrin
Designer
 Jeff Fisher

Michael C. Johnson
Director of Information Systems

Direct: 425/893-5061 • Fax: 425/893-5056
e-mail: michaelj@seahawks.com

11220 NE 53rd Street
Kirkland, WA 98033
425/827-9777

d Street
98033

11220 NE 53rd Street • Kirkland, WA 98033 • 425/827-9777 • www.seahawks.com

Client
Seattle Seahawks
Design Firm
Jeff Fisher LogoMotives
(continued)

Seattle Seahawks

SPONSORSHIP OPPORTUNITIES

Kingdome Signage

Publications/Print

**Seahawks On-Line/
WWW.seahawks.com**

...cast Opportunities

...Day Event Sponsorships

...nity Outreach/
...Marketing

...ks Training Camp

...orporate Hospitality
...pportunities

66 Our spons...
package with ...
Seahawks cor...
an excellent b...
of media, sign...
and corporate
hospitality. Xe...
is pleased to be ...
Official Docume...
Technology Con...
of the Seahawks...
to be associated ...
an organization t...
helps us to meet ...
regional advertis...
objectives. 99

*Elizabeth Bangasser
Director pf Marketing
Xerox Corporation*

Seattle Seahawks

PUBLICAT

The Seahawks publish se
with statistics and inform
entertain our football fan
company tremendous opp
Seahawks fans.

Tailgate Times
This is the advertising p
for the Seahawks Tailga
piece is distributed befo
game to fans attending t
Circulation is 15,000 per

GameDay Magazine
This magazine is produc
each Seahawks home ga
rosters, player and oppo
much more. It is a boun
and white and color adve
10,000 per game plus ar

Seahawks Pocket Sched
Pocket Schedules are pro
contain the Seahawks u
are an excellent vehicle
the entire Seahawks reg
hands of this desirable c
throughout the year tim
printed on quantities of
to 1 million.

Other print advertising
eahawks include the S
ide, Season Ticket H
ason Ticket Holder Qu
me day flip cards and
ets.

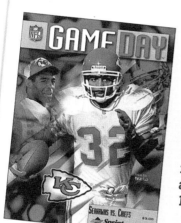

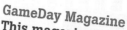

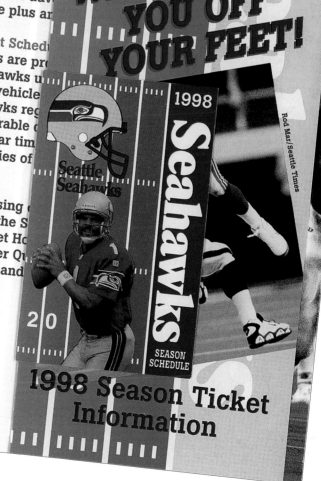

TOTAL ENTERTAINER AND ATHLETE MANAGEMENT
6514 Riverview Lane, Dallas, Texas 75248-2854
direct: 972-931-8617 mobile: 972-679-6171 fax: 972-931-8618
e-mail: agentsaw@aol.com website: www.teaam.com

Steven A. Weinberg, Esq.
Chief Executive Officer

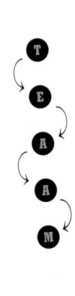

244

TOTAL ENTERTAINER AND ATHLETE MANAGEMENT

6514 Riverview Lane, Dallas, Texas 75248

tel 972-931-8617 / 800-478-9811 fax 972-931-8618 www.teaam.com

DIGITAL STUDIO ▪ 1700 K Street NW, Suite 1200 ▪ Washington, DC 20006

PRINTING AND FINISHING ▪ 4812 Lawrence Street ▪ Hyattsville, Maryland 20781

omnigraphics

omnigraphics

Digital Studio

1700 K Street NW
Suite 1200
Washington
DC 20006

Phone
202-785-9605

Fax
202-785-9609

BBS
202-785-9610

Printing & Finishing

4812 Lawrence Street
Hyattsville
Maryland 20781

Phone
301-277-8805

Toll-Free
800-797-6664

Fax
301-277-8357

Client
Omnigraphics
Design Firm
Dever Designs
Laurel, Maryland
Designer
Jeffrey L. Dever

omnigraphics

omnigraphics

246

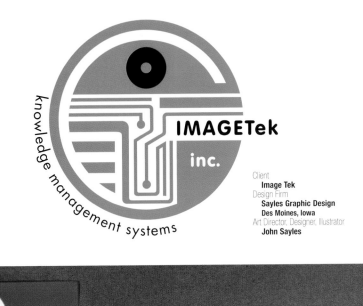

IMAGETek
inc.

knowledge management systems

Client
Image Tek
Design Firm
Sayles Graphic Design
Des Moines, Iowa
Art Director, Designer, Illustrator
John Sayles

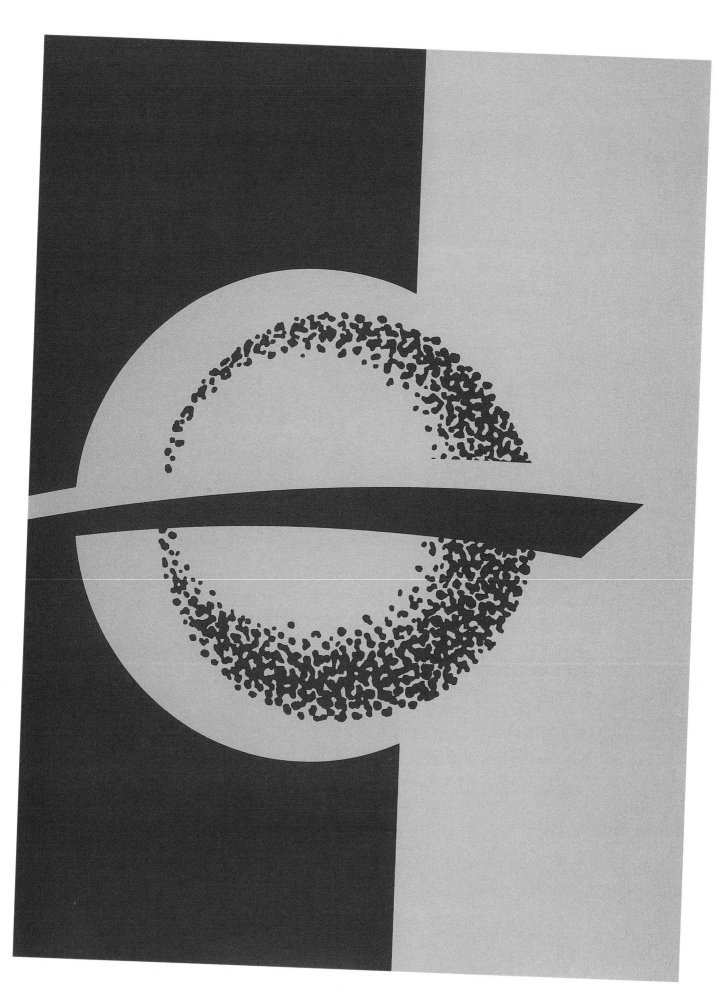

Client
**Carnegie Endowment
for International Peace**
Design Firm
**Dever Designs
Laurel, Maryland**
Designers
**Jeffrey L. Dever,
Emily Martin Kendall**

Thomas W. Skladony
Director of Publications

CARNEGIE ENDOWMENT
for International Peace

1779 Massachusetts Ave., NW
Washington, DC 20036
202-939-2217
Fax 202-483-1840
skladony@ceip.org

CARNEGIE ENDOWMENT
for International Peace

Jessica T. Mathews
President

CARNEGIE ENDOWMENT
for International Peace

With compliments of
Jessica Tuchman Mathews
President

1779 Massachusetts Avenue, NW ■ Washington, DC 20036
Phone 202-939-2210 ■ Fax 202-332-0925 ■ jmathews@ceip.org

RNEGIE ENDOWMENT
for International Peace

1779 Massachusetts Avenue, NW, Washington, DC 20036
Phone 202-939-2210 ■ Fax 202-332-0925 ■ jmathews@ceip.org ■ www.ceip.org

CARNEGIE ENDOWMENT
for International Peace

Where
Pioneering
nds

Sherry Pettie
Production Editor

CARNEGIE ENDOWMENT
for International Peace

1779 Massachusetts Ave., NW
Washington, DC 20036
202-939-2226
Fax **202-483-1840**
spettie@ceip.org

Client
**Carnegie Endowment
for International Peace**
Design Firm
Dever Designs
(continued)

251

Client
1997 Iowa State Fair "Go For It"
Design Firm
Sayles Graphic Design
Des Moines, Iowa
Art Director, Designer, Illustrator
John Sayles

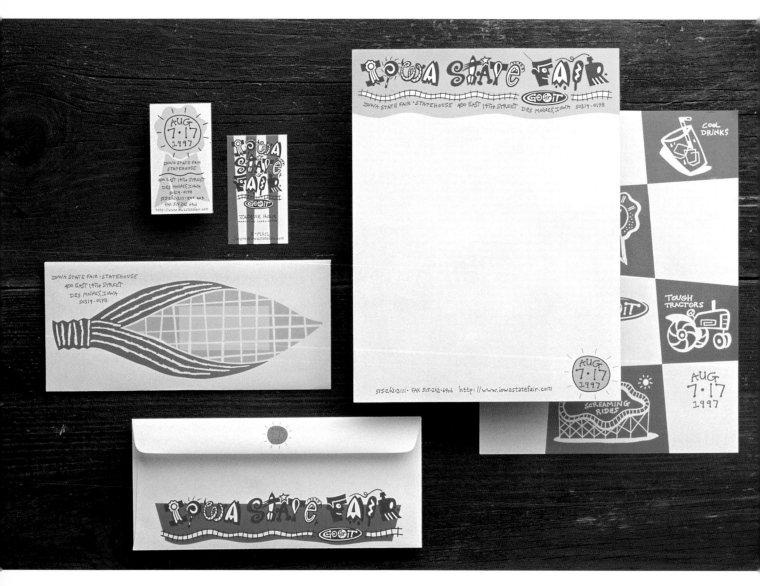

Client
etrieve
Design Firm
Hornall Anderson Design Works, Inc.
Seattle, Washington
Designers
John Hornall, Kathy Saito,
Henry Yiu, Andrew Smith

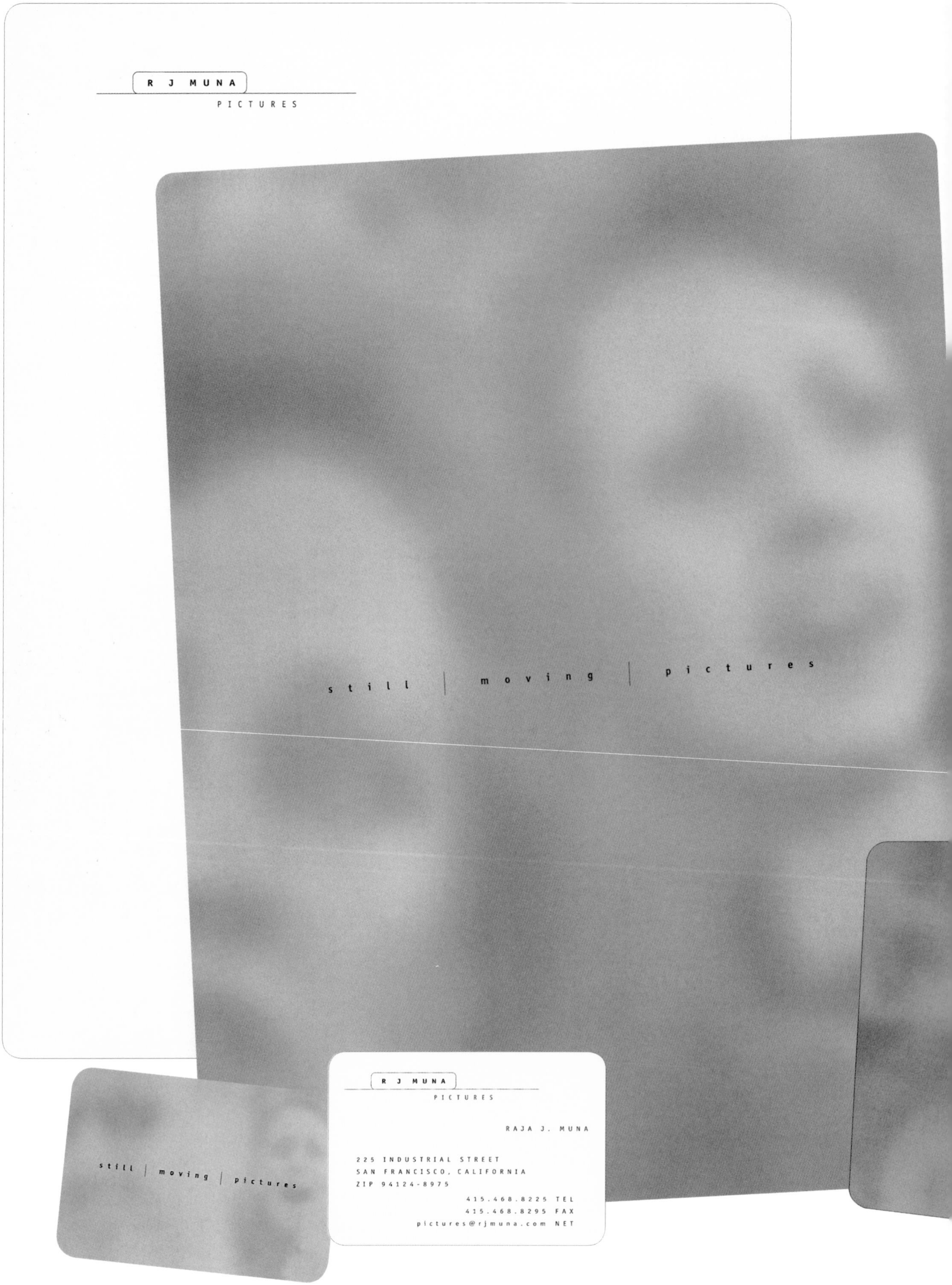

still | moving | pictures

still | moving | pictures

Client
RJ Muna
Design Firm
AERIAL
San Francisco, California
Designer
Tracy Moon

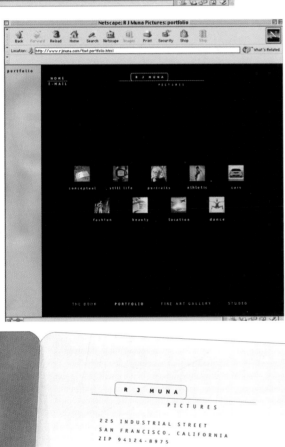

Client
Oxbow
Design Firm
Rick Johnson & Company
Albuquerque, New Mexico
Designer
Tim McGrath

JIM ROGERS
DEVELOPER

8110 LOMAS NE
ALBUQUERQUE, N.M. 87110
TEL: 505.265.8996
FAX: 505.265.8997

P.O. DRAWER AA ALBUQUERQUE, N.M. 87103 TEL: 505.265.8996 FAX: 505.265.8997

P.O. DRAWER AA ALBUQUERQUE, N.M.

Client
Oxbow
Design Firm
Rick Johnson & Company
(continued)

8110 Lomas NE Albuquerque, N.M. 87110

OXBOW

8110 Lomas NE Albuquerque, N.M. 87110

JIM ROGERS
DEVELOPER

8110 Lomas NE
Albuquerque, N.M. 87110
Tel: 505.265.8996
Fax: 505.265.8997

grape finds

www.grapefinds.com

Theodore Adamstein
Partner

GrapeFinds, Inc.
1643 Connecticut Avenue
Washington, DC 20009
tel: 202.387.3146
fax: 202.387.7874
tadamstein@grapefinds.com
www.grapefinds.com

grape finds

1643 Connecticut Avenue, Washington, DC 20009 ph:

Client
Grapefinds
Design Firm
**Hornall Anderson
Design Works, Inc.
Seattle, Washington**
Designers
**Jack Anderson, Lisa Cerveny,
Mary Chin Hutchison,
Gretchen Cook**

grape finds

grape finds

Client
Peggy Sundays
Design Firm
Jeff Fisher LogoMotives
Portland, Oregon
Designer
Jeff Fisher

7880 SW Capitol Hwy. • Portland, OR 97219

Phone: **503/246-8263** • Fax: 503/768 -3969

7880 SW Capitol Hwy.
Portland, OR 97219

Home Essentials in Multnomah Village

*Home Essentials in
Multnomah Village*

Peggy Seaman

7880 SW Capitol Hwy.
Portland, OR 97219

Phone: **503/246-8263**
Fax: 503/768 -3969

Client
violet.com
Design Firm
AERIAL
San Francisco, California
Designers
Tracy Moon,
Stephanie West

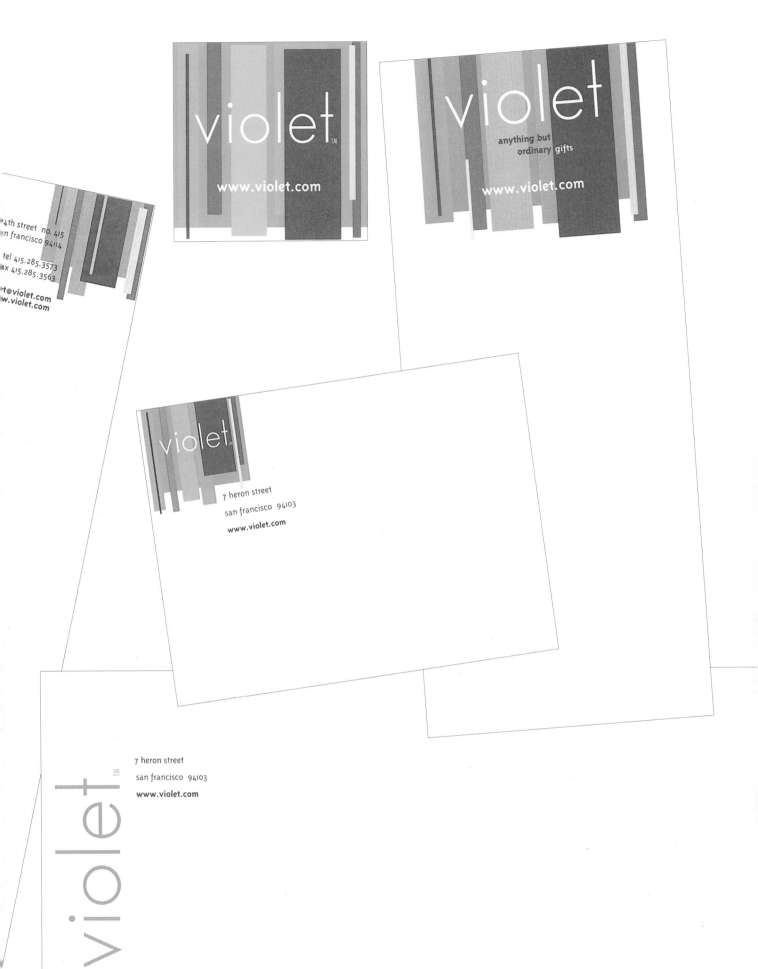

violet ™
www.violet.com

violet ™
anything but
ordinary gifts
www.violet.com

4th street no. 415
n francisco 94114

tel 415.285.3573
ax 415.285.3563

t@violet.com
w.violet.com

violet ™
7 heron street
san francisco 94103
www.violet.com

violet ™
7 heron street
san francisco 94103
www.violet.com

Client
Space Needle
Design Firm
Hornall Anderson Design Works, Inc.
Seattle, Washington
Designers
Jack Anderson, Mary Hermes,
Gretchen Cook, Andrew Smith,
Alan Florsheim

space needle

S K I N N E R

PROFESSIONAL LAW CORPORATION

Client
Skinner Law
Design Firm
Heart Graphic Design
Midland, Michigan
Designer
Clark Most

S K I N N E R

PROFESSIONAL LAW CORPORATION

S K I N N E R

PROFESSIONAL LAW CORPORATION

R I C H A R D F E E L E Y

A T T O R N E Y

1 0 1 F I R S T   S U I T E 1 0 5
P O S T O F F I C E B O X 9 8
B A Y C I T Y M I 4 8 7 0 7 - 0 0 9 8
T E L E P H O N E : 5 1 7 8 9 3 5 5 4 7
F A C S I M I L E : 5 1 7 8 9 3 5 5 4 9
E-MAIL: richard@skinnerlex.com

S K I N N E R

PROFESSIONAL LAW CORPORATION

1 0 1 F I R S T · S U I T E 1 0 5
P O S T O F F I C E B O X 9 8
B A Y C I T Y , M I 4 8 7 0 7 - 0 0 9 8

1 0 1 F I R S T · S U I T E 1 0 5
P O S T O F F I C E B O X 9 8
B A Y C I T Y , M I 4 8 7 0 7 - 0 0 9 8
T E L E P H O N E : 5 1 7 8 9 3 5 5 4 9
F A C S I M I L E : 5 1 7 8 9 3 5 5 4 9
E-MAIL: info@skinnerlex.com

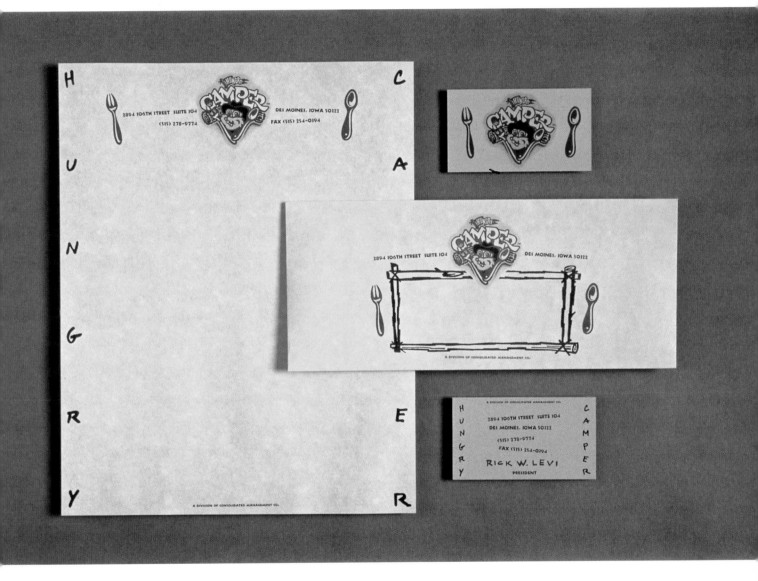

Client
Hungry Camper
Design Firm
Sayles Graphic Design
Des Moines, Iowa
Art Director, Designer, Illustrator
John Sayles

UNIVERSITY INN
AND CONFERENCE CENTER
AT RUTGERS

RUTGERS, THE STATE UNIVERSITY OF NEW JERSEY

UNIVERSITY INN
AND CONFERENCE CENTER
AT RUTGERS

Client
University Inn & Conference Center
Design Firm
Rutgers University Publications
New Brunswick, New Jersey
Designer
John Van Cleaf

UNIVERSITY INN
AND CONFERENCE CENTER
AT RUTGERS

UNIVERSITY INN

and Conference Center at Rutgers

Rutgers, The State University of New Jersey
178 Ryders Lane
New Brunswick, NJ 08901-8556

Conferences and Events: **732/932-9148**
Room Reservations: **732/932-9144**
Email: **univinn@rci.rutgers.edu**
Website: **http://univinn.rutgers.edu**

UNIVERSITY INN
AND CONFERENCE CENTER
AT RUTGERS

Rutgers, The State University of New Jersey • 79 Clifton Avenue • New Brunswick, NJ 08901-8535

Rutgers, The State University of New Jersey • 79 Clifton Avenue • New Brunswick, NJ 08901-8535
732/932-9144 • Fax: 732/932-6952
Email: univinn@rci.rutgers.edu

UNIVERSITY INN
AND CONFERENCE CENTER
AT RUTGERS

Rutgers, The State University
of New Jersey
79 Clifton Avenue
New Brunswick, NJ 08901-8535
732/932-9144
Fax: 732/932-6952
Email: univinn@rci.rutgers.edu

UNIVERSITY INN
AND CONFERENCE CENTER
AT RUTGERS

Rutgers, The State University of New Jersey
79 Clifton Avenue
New Brunswick, NJ 08901-8535

GINA E. BELLITTI
Business Manager

Rutgers, The State University of New Jersey
178 Ryders Lane
New Brunswick, NJ 08901-8556
Voice: 732/932-9767
Fax: 732/932-1641
Email: gbellit@rci.rutgers.edu
Website: http://univinn.rutgers.edu

UNIVERSITY INN
AND CONFERENCE CENTER
AT RUTGERS

Client
**University Inn &
Conference Center**
Design Firm
**Rutgers University
Publications**
(continued)

UNIVERSITY INN
ND CONFERENCE C
T RUTGERS

*A charming getaway...inside a full-service
conference center*

When your conference is over for the day, relax into the restful
fully landscaped
a mini-vacation

ed parkland, yet
nd Internet access.
University Inn is
e and again.

niversity
ing and
-use

UNIVERSITY INN
AND CONFERENCE CENTER
AT RUTGERS

beautiful...wired...

and easy on

the budget too...

Client
Mr. Reynold's Limousine Service
Design Firm
Sayles Graphic Design
Des Moines, Iowa
Art Director, Designer, Illustrator
John Sayles

WHO IS MR. REYNOLDS? HE'S YOUR CHAUFFEUR! THE REYNOLDS FAMILY IS COMMITTED TO YOUR SATISFACTION. WE PROMISE IMPECCABLE SERVICE AND A CLEAN STRETCH LIMOUSINE EVERY TIME!

Client
La Parisienne
Design Firm
Bjornson Design Associates, Inc.
Philadelphia, Pennsylvania
Designer
Jon Anders Bjornson

gettuit.com

Client
Gettuit.com
Design Firm
Hornall Anderson Design Works, Inc.
Seattle, Washington
Designers
Jack Anderson, Kathy Saito,
Henry Yiu, Alan Copeland,
Gretchen Cook

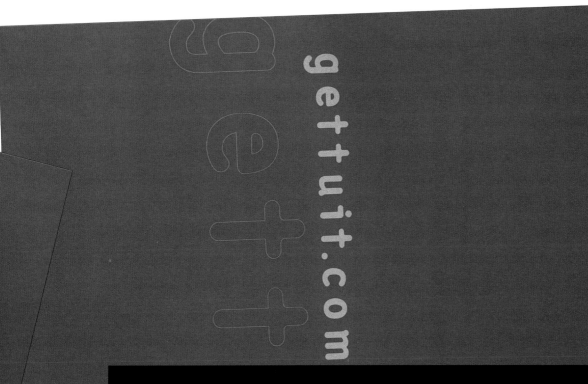

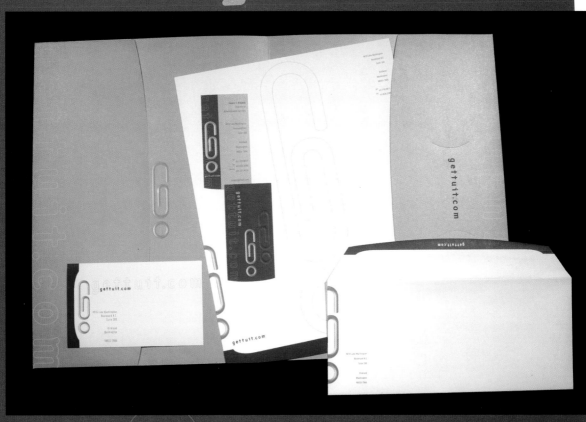

4010 Lake Washington
Boulevard N.E.
Suite 300

Kirkland
Washington
98033-7866

www.gettuit.com
info@gettuit.com

gettuit.com

RUNET 2000

RUTGERS, THE STATE UNIVERSITY OF NEW JERSEY

R U N E T 2 0 0 0

RUNET 2000
RUTGERS, THE STATE UNIVERSITY OF NEW JERSEY
63 ROAD 1
PISCATAWAY, NEW JERSEY 08854-8031

RUNET 2000
RUTGERS, THE STATE UNIVERSITY
OF NEW JERSEY

63 ROAD 1

PISCATAWAY, NEW JERSEY
08854-8031

732/445-1470

THE STATE UNIVERSITY OF NEW JERSEY
RUTGERS

Client
   RUNet 2000
Design Firm
   Rutgers University Publications
   New Brunswick, New Jersey
Designer
   John Van Cleaf

R U N E T 2 0 0 0

RUNet 2000
Room 264 • Hill Center • Busch Campus
Rutgers, The State University of New Jersey
Computing Services
110 Frelinghuysen Road
Piscataway, New Jersey 08854-8089

732/445-2743
FAX: 732/445-5539

RUNET 2000

Client
RUNet 2000
Design Firm
**Rutgers University
Publications**
(continued)

http://runet2000.rutgers.

RUTGERS, THE STATE UNIVERSITY OF NEW JERSE

t2000.rutgers.edu

TE UNIVERSITY OF NEW JERSEY

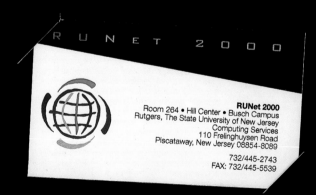

R U N E T 2 0 0 0

RUNet 2000
Room 264 • Hill Center • Busch Campus
Rutgers, The State University of New Jersey
Computing Services
110 Frelinghuysen Road
Piscataway, New Jersey 08854-8089

732/445-2743
FAX: 732/445-5539

R U N E T   2 0 0 0

BUILDING AN INFORMATION INFRASTRUCTURE:

An Introduction for
Faculty and Staff

RUNET 2000

BUILDING AN
INFORMATION
INFRASTRUCTURE

R U N E T   2 0 0 0

BUILDING AN INFORMATION INFRASTRUCTURE

HTTP://RUNET2000.RUTGERS.EDU

Client
1998 Iowa State Fair "Way Too Much Fun!"
Design Firm
Sayles Graphic Design
Des Moines, Iowa
Art Director, Designer, Illustrator
John Sayles

Client
Rick Johnson
& Company
Design Firm
Rick Johnson
& Company
Albuquerque, New Mexico
Designer
Lisa Graff

RICK JOHNSON & COMPANY

A D V E R T I S I N G

RICK JOHNSON & COMPANY

A D V E R T I S I N G

RICK JOHNSON & COMPANY

A D V E R T I S I N G

Tim McGrath, Designer
1120 Pennsylvania NE, Albuquerque, NM 87110
phone **505-266-1100** | *fax* **505-262-0525** | *e-mail* tmcgrath@rjc.com

1120 Pennsylvania NE, PO Box 4770, Albuquerque, NM 87196

RICK JOHNSON & COMPANY

A D V E R T I S I N G

1120 Pennsylvania NE, PO Box 4770, Albuquerque, NM 87196 | *phone* 505-266-1100 | *fax* 505-262-0525
Offices in Arizona, New Mexico, Texas

1120 Pennsylvania NE, PO Box 4770, Albuquerque, NM 87196

RICK JOHNSON & COMPANY

602 West 1st Street

Tempe, Arizona 85281-2606

CORKY HOUCHARD
PRESIDENT
CELL: 602-620-3203

602 West 1st Street Tempe, Arizona 85281-2606

TEL: 480-966-9600 EXT 124 FAX: 480-966-4100

EMAIL: chouchard@mcwholdings.com

602 West 1st Street Tempe, Arizona 85281-2606 TEL: 480-966-4400 FAX: 480-966-2299

Client
Brownstone Residential
Design Firm
Sullivan Marketing & Communications
Phoenix, Arizona
Designer
Jack Sullivan

Paris
LAS VEGAS

A HILTON CASINO RESORT

Client
Paris Casino Resort
Design Firm
David Carter Design Assoc.
Dallas, Texas
Stationery Designer
Ashley Barron
Logo Designer
R&R Advertising in Las Vegas

VIVE LA FRANCE

LA JOIE DE VIVRE

vive las vegas

PARIS LAS VEGAS
3655 Las Vegas Boulevard, South
Las Vegas, Nevada 89109

PARIS LAS VEGAS
3655 Las Vegas Boulevard, South
Las Vegas, Nevada 89109
Telephone 702.946.7000
Facsimile 702.946.4405

VIRTUOSO

SPECIALISTS IN THE ART OF TRAVEL

Client
Virtuoso
Design Firm
David Carter Design Assoc.
Dallas, Texas
Art Director
Ashley Barron
Designers
Ashley Barron, Tabitha Bogard,
Melissa Pattison

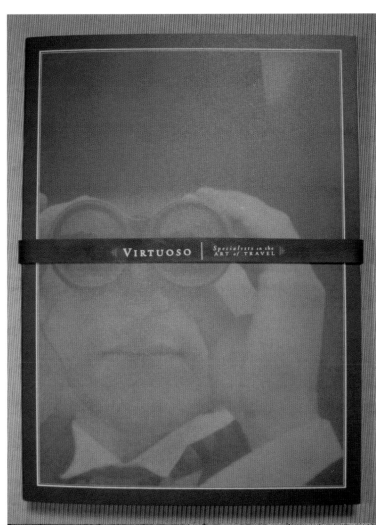

VIRTUOSO

SPECIALISTS IN THE ART OF TRAVEL

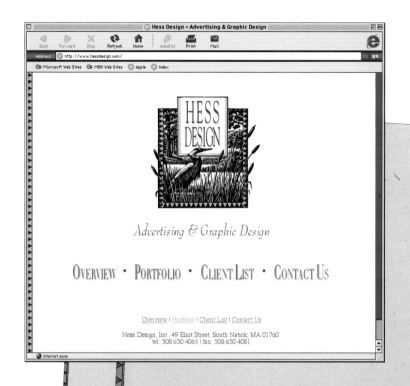

Hess Design, Inc.

49 Eliot Street
South Natick
Massachusetts
0 1 7 6 0

Advertising &
Graphic Design

8B Pleasant Street
South Natick
Massachusetts
0 1 7 6 0

508 . 650 . 4063
Fax 508 . 650 . 4081

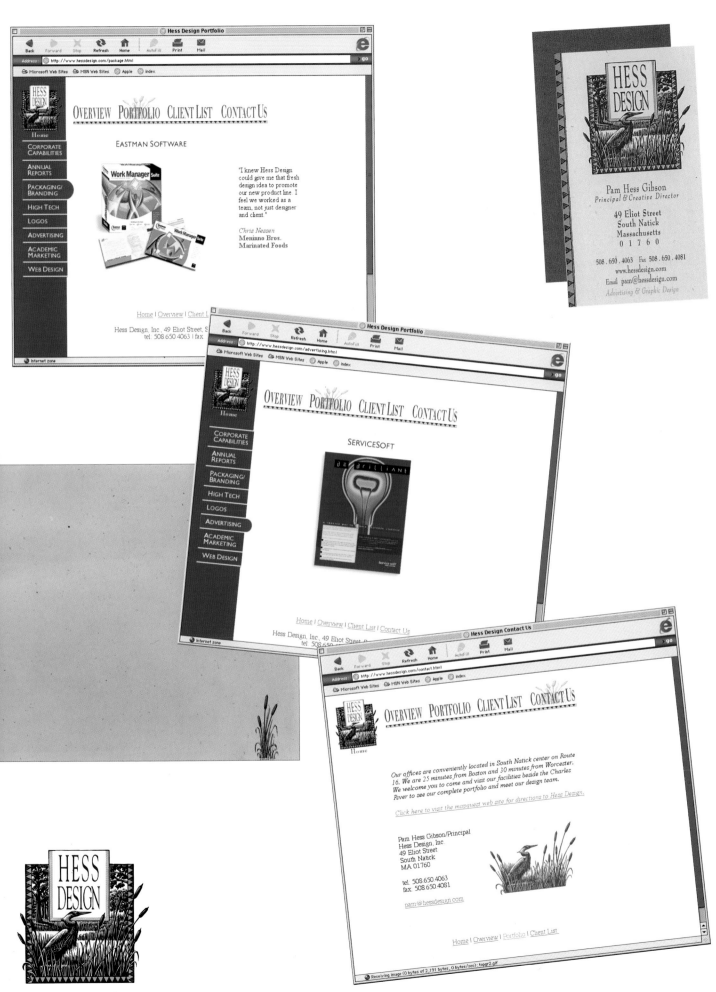

OVERVIEW PORTFOLIO CLIENT LIST CONTACT US

Home

CORPORATE CAPABILITIES

ANNUAL REPORTS

PACKAGING/ BRANDING

HIGH TECH

LOGOS

ADVERTISING

ACADEMIC MARKETING

WEB DESIGN

EASTMAN SOFTWARE

"I knew Hess Design could give me that fresh design idea to promote our new product line. I feel we worked as a team, not just designer and client."

Chris Nessen
Meninno Bros.
Marinated Foods

Home | Overview | Client L

Hess Design, Inc., 49 Eliot Street, S
tel. 508 650 4063 | fax

OVERVIEW PORTFOLIO CLIENT LIST CONTACT US

Home

CORPORATE CAPABILITIES

ANNUAL REPORTS

PACKAGING/ BRANDING

HIGH TECH

LOGOS

ADVERTISING

ACADEMIC MARKETING

WEB DESIGN

SERVICESOFT

Home | Overview | Client List | Contact Us

Hess Design, Inc., 49 Eliot Street, S
tel. 508 650

HESS DESIGN

Pam Hess Gibson
Principal & Creative Director

49 Eliot Street
South Natick
Massachusetts
0 1 7 6 0

508 . 650 . 4063 Fax 508 . 650 . 4081
www.hessdesign.com
Email pam@hessdesign.com

Advertising & Graphic Design

OVERVIEW PORTFOLIO CLIENT LIST CONTACT US

Home

Our offices are conveniently located in South Natick center on Route 16. We are 25 minutes from Boston and 30 minutes from Worcester. We welcome you to come and visit our facilities beside the Charles River to see our complete portfolio and meet our design team.

Click here to visit the mapquest web site for directions to Hess Design.

Pam Hess Gibson/Principal
Hess Design, Inc.
49 Eliot Street
South Natick
MA 01760

tel. 508 650 4063
fax. 508 650 4081

pam@hessdesign.com

Home | Overview | Portfolio | Client List

HESS DESIGN

Client
Care Future
Design Firm
Hornall Anderson Design Works, Inc.
Seattle, Washington
Designers
John Hornall, Jana Wilson Esser,
Hillary Radbill, Sonja Max,
Michael Brugman

care**Future**

care**Future**
3605 NE 18th Street · Portland,

Client
The City
Design Firm
William Homan Design
Richfield, Minnesota
Designer
William Homan

SAM
GURNOE
DIRECTOR
INDIAN RESOURCE
POOL

612-724-3689

THE CITY, INC.
1545 EAST LAKE STREET
MINNEAPOLIS, MINNESOTA
55407

1545

EAST

LAKE

STREET

MINNEAPOLIS

MINNESOTA

55407

THE CITY, INC.
1545 EAST LAKE STREET
MINNEAPOLIS, MINNESOTA
55407

THE CITY, INC.
1545 EAST LAKE STREET
MINNEAPOLIS, MN 55407

612-724-3689

THE CITY

THE CITY

THE CITY, INC
1545 EAST LAKE ST
MINNEAPOLIS, MIN
55407

IF YOU
VISIT
US
HINK
L

Client
The City
Design Firm
**William Homan
Design**
(continued)

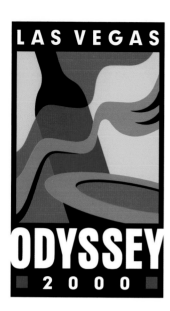

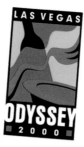

A celebration
of wine, food
and art ■ ■ ■

Client
Las Vegas Odyssey
Design Firm
Tusk Studios
Las Vegas, Nevada
Designers
Debra Heiser,
Virginia Thompson, Scott Wizell
HTML Programming
Style Wise Interactive

T 702.257.2345
F 702.257.2501
877.370.9182
p.o. box 27349
las vegas, nv
89126-1349 ■ ■

TO:

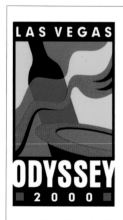

p.o. box 27349
las vegas, nv
89126-1349 ■ ■

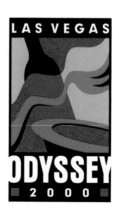

■ THANK YOU ■

Back Forward Reload Home Search Netscape Images Print Security Shop Stop

Location: http://www.lasvegasodyssey.com/index.html   What's Related

[Image]

LAS VEGAS
ODYSSEY 2000
A celebration of wine, food and art ■ ■ ■

ODYSSEY
EVENT SCHEDULE
PURCHASE
ACCOMMODATIONS
CHEFS
SOMMELIERS
VINTNERS
RESTAURANTS
AUCTION LOTS

an appetizing four-day event

Closing out the 20th century, as only Las Vegas could, the entertainment capital brought the attention of the world to its doorstep with the creation of unparalleled, awe-inspiring resorts such as Bellagio, Mandalay Bay, The Regent Las Vegas and the Venetian. And some of the best chefs and restaurants on the planet joined these and other established properties such as the Mirage, Rio, MGM Grand, Desert Inn and Monte Carlo to create a culinary oasis in the desert.

Now, in the year 2000, in recognition of the city's unique culinary talents, Las Vegas Odyssey, in conjunction with Archie McLaren, founding director of KCBX Central Coast Wine Classic, will present a first-ever for Las Vegas: Las Vegas Odyssey 2000: A Celebration of Wine, Food and Art, hosted by Las Vegas' newest spectacular attraction, the Aladdin Resort & Casino.

Through Odyssey 2000, Las Vegas can now pay tribute to the most renowned names in the culinary world during its four-day event. Las Vegas Odyssey 2000 will donate a portion of the proceeds to public television KLVX Channel 10.

In some of Las Vegas' finest properties and restaurants, Odyssey 2000 will showcase exceptional artwork from local and national artists to complement the extraordinary cuisine and fine wines. Las Vegas' foremost chefs and sommeliers will host and present varied wine tastings, a caviar and champagne tasting at the House of Blues Foundation Room, dinners, a blues brunch and unprecedented cooking demonstrations by world-class chefs in their very own restaurants.

October 26 to 29, Las Vegas Odyssey 2000:
A Celebration of Wine, Food and Art

CLICK HERE TO TAKE A PEEK AT SOME OF THE SPECTACULAR MENUS
OUR CHEFS HAVE CREATED FOR LAS VEGAS ODYSSEY 2000!

ODYSSEY 2000 PLATINUM SPONSORS

tusk STUDIOS   Williamson Printing   FoodLine   Think Inc.

ODYSSEY 2000 GOLD SPONSORS

Sotheby's   C&S SALES

ODYSSEY 2000 SILVER SPONSORS

WINE JOURNAL   WHERE

Event subject to change including chefs, sommeliers, and restaurants. Ticket prices may vary. Seating is limited.

© Tusk Studios   ABOUT US   SPONSORSHIP OPPORTUNITIES   CONTACT US   VIEW ITEMS IN YOUR SHOPPING CART

Back Forward Reload Home Search Netscape Images Print Security Shop Stop

Location: http://www.lasvegasodyssey.com/index.html   What's Related

[Image]

LAS VEGAS
ODYSSEY 2000
A celebration of wine, food and art ■ ■ ■

ODYSSEY
EVENT SCHEDULE
PURCHASE
ACCOMMODATIONS
CHEFS
SOMMELIERS
VINTNERS
RESTAURANTS
AUCTION LOTS

las vegas' finest restaurants

CHINOIS
Asian/American/French. Located in The Forum Shops at Caesars. Cafe-style, indoor and "outdoor" seating. Dishes served family-style. Exposition kitchen and sushi bar. House specialties include Shanghai lobster, whole sizzling catfish, grilled Mongolian Lamb and Hog Island oysters on the half shell. Excellent wine list.

ELEMENTS
Elegant and contemporary, Elements is the Aladdin Resort & Casino's signature restaurant. It features a tantalizing mix of dishes created from fire and water: fresh seafood, prime cuts of selected corn-fed beef and pastas, plus an extensive wine list.

GATSBY'S
Asian/French California-style. Located in MGM Grand. Elegant decor. Daily rotation of dishes and specialty entrées. House specialties included seasonal terrines, sautéed Dover sole, sweetbreads with fresh Hudson Valley foie gras, grilled ostrich with wild mushroom risotto, genuine Kobe beef. Outstanding wine selection.

HOUSE OF BLUES
Southern-inspired, regional cuisine includes Creole/Cajun fare such a jambalaya, gumbo, Southern fried catfish, wood-fired pizza, barbecued ribs and "Blues" burgers. Located in Mandalay Bay. This casual atmosphere features a vast collection of folk art. Sunday Gospel Brunch showcases gospel music and all-you-can-eat Southern style buffet.

PREVIOUS NEXT

© Tusk Studios   ABOUT US   SPONSORSHIP OPPORTUNITIES   CONTACT US   VIEW ITEMS IN YOUR SHOPPING CART

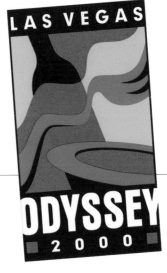

LAS VEGAS
ODYSSEY 2000

A celebration
of wine, food
and art ■ ■ ■

Debra Heiser
principal

702.257.2345
702.257.2501
p.o. box 27349
las vegas, nv
89126-1349 ■ ■
www.lasvegasodyssey.com

LAS VEGAS
ODYSSEY 2000

p.o. box 27349
las vegas, nv
89126-1349 ■ ■

Client
Las Vegas Odyssey
Design Firm
Tusk Studios
(continued)

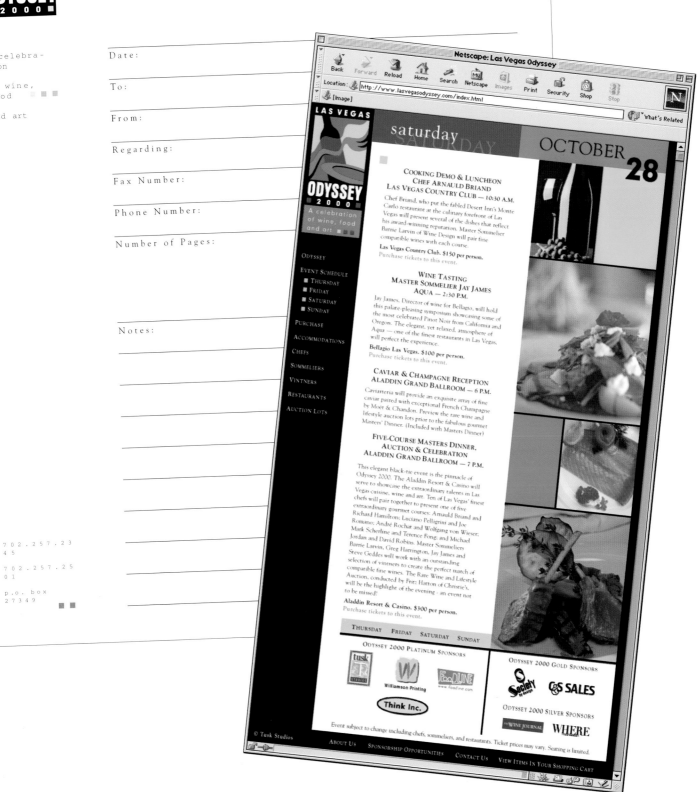

Client
The Finishing Touch
Design Firm
Sayles Graphic Design
Des Moines, Iowa
Art Director, Designer
John Sayles

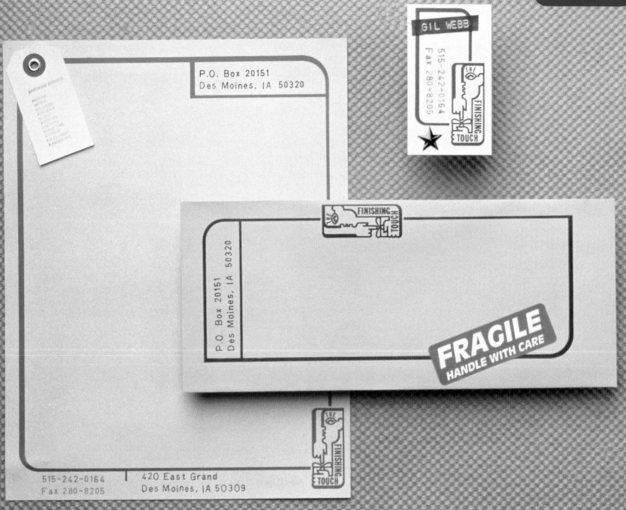

1000 St.Louis Union Station Suite 100 St.Louis MO 63103

Call 314 621.7678
POST
or
Fax 314 621.8800

PROVIDING

GREAT Service
+
SUPERIOR STAFF
+
STATE OF THE ART Facilities

OUR STAFF, Service and STATE OF THE ART Facilities Will Keep You On The FAST TRACK

First Class
Audio & Video POST Production

Client
Grand Central Post
Design Firm
Phoenix Creative
St. Louis, Missouri
Designer
Ed Mantels-Seeker

Mike Luhning
3D Animator

Call 314 621.7678
POST
or
Fax 314 621.8800

1000 St.Louis Union Station Suite 100

St.Louis MO 63103

1000 St.Louis Union Station Suite 100 St.Louis MO 63103

299

GOVERNOR
HOTEL

S.W. Tenth at Alder
Portland, Oregon 97205

GOVERNOR
HOTEL

S.W. Tenth at Alder
Portland, Oregon 97205

Client
Governor Hotel
Design Firm
Jeff Fisher LogoMotives
Portland, Oregon
Creative Director
Mary Jo McCloskey
Designer
Jeff Fisher

GOVERNOR
HOTEL

THE GOVERNOR REQUESTS YOUR PRESENCE.

S.W. Tenth at Alder, Portland, Oregon 97205 · 503/224-3400 1/800/554-3456 Fax 503/

Operated by Salishan Lodge, also operators of The Salish Lodge and Skamania Lodge

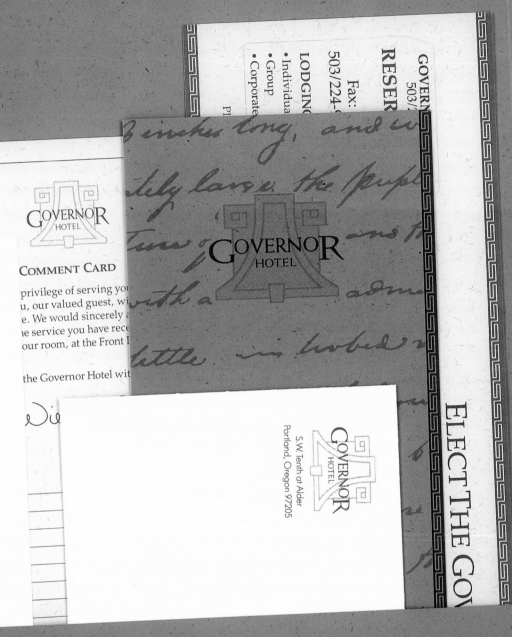

GOVERNOR
HOTEL

COMMENT CARD

privilege of serving you
u, our valued guest, wi
e. We would sincerely a
e service you have rece
our room, at the Front D

the Governor Hotel wit

GOVERNOR
HOTEL

S.W. Tenth at Alder
Portland, Oregon 97205

RESER
503/
Fax:
503/224-
LODGIN
• Individua
• Group
• Corporate

ELECT THE GO

GOVERNOR
HOTEL

S.W. Tenth at Alder   Portland, Oregon 97205
503/224-3400   Fax 503/224-9426

Client
Governor Hotel
Design Firm
 Jeff Fisher LogoMotives
(continued)

GOVERNOR HOTEL

MEETING AND BANQUET FA

Our spe
selection
accommo
to 600
Ball
sign
and
imp
bea
ceil
mor

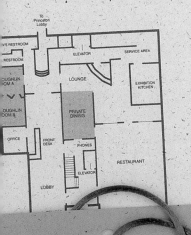

GOVERNOR HOTEL

Sharon Grosse
Sales Manager

S.W. Tenth at Alder, Portland, Oregon 97205
503/241-2101   1/800/554-3456   Fax 503/224-9426
*Operated by Salishan Lodge, also operators of
The Salish Lodge and Skamania Lodge*

Just Married.
Do Not
Disturb.

Lynn Ridenour
Director of
Corporate
Communications
425.519.9313
lynnr@onyx.com

310-120th Ave NE
Bellevue, WA 98005
(T) 425.451.8060
(F) 425.519.4002
www.onyx.com

Client
Onyx Software
Design Firm
**Hornall Anderson Design Works, Inc.
Seattle, Washington**
Designers
**John Hornall, Debra McCloskey,
Holly Craven, Jana Wilson Esser**

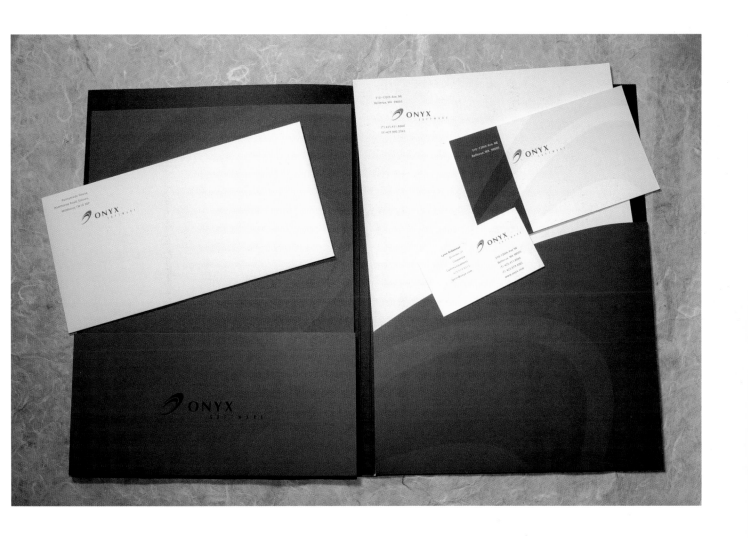

10 Munson Street | LeRoy, New York 14482 | (716) 768-2561 | Fax (716) 768-4335

LeRoy Village Green
RESIDENTIAL HEALTHCARE FACILITY

Your answer to long-term care and short-term rehabilitation.™
An affiliate of the Bartholomew Healthcare Group

10 Munson Street, LeRoy, NY 14482
(716)768-2561 Fax (716)768-4335
www.leroyvillagegreen.com

Equal Housing Opportunity

Client
LeRoy Village Green
Design Firm
McElveney & Palozzi
Design Group Inc.
Rochester, New York
Creative Director
William McElveney
Art Director
Lisa Parenti
Designer
Jan Marie Gallagher

BLÖCH+COULTER
Design Group

2440 S. Sepulveda Blvd., #152

Los Angeles, California 90064

Telephone (310) 445-6550

Facsimile (310) 445-6555

admin@blochcoulter.com

www.blochcoulter.com

BLÖCH+COULTER
Design Group

BLÖCH+COULTER
Design Group

2440 S. Sepulveda Blvd., #152

Los Angeles, California 90064

Telephone (310) 445-6550

Facsimile (310) 445-6555

admin@blochcoulter.com

www.blochcoulter.com

BLÖCH+COULTER
Design Group

2440 S. Sepulveda Blvd., #152
Los Angeles, California 90064

Invoice

Date

Client PO

☐ Resale

Project Description

Professional Services

2440 S. Sepulveda Blvd., #152
Los Angeles, California 90064
Telephone (310) 445-6550
Facsimile (310) 445-6555
admin@blochcoulter.com
www.blochcoulter.com

BLÖCH+COULTER
Design Group

VICTORIA COULTER
2440 S. Sepulveda Blvd., #152
Los Angeles, California 90064
Telephone (310) 445-6550
Facsimile (310) 445-6555
victoria@blochcoulter.com
www.blochcoulter.com

Strategic Graphic Design

Since 1970

ANNUAL REPORTS

BROCHURES

CATALOGS

IDENTITIES/BRANDING

PACKAGING

WEB SITES

st Due

Client
Bloch + Coulter
Design Group
Design Firm
Bloch + Coulter
Design Group
Los Angeles, California
Designers
Ellie Young Suh,
Thomas Bloch

Diplomate American Board of Oral
and Maxillofacial Surgery

Fellow American College of Surgeons

American Dental Association

American Medical Association

REED H. DAY, M.D., D.M.D., F.A.C.S.

ORAL & FACIAL
SURGERY CENTER

REED H. DAY, M.D., D.M.D., F.A.C.S.

2222 E. Highland Ave., Suite #320
Phoenix, AZ 85016

6200 S. McClintock Dr., Suite #6A
Tempe, AZ 85283

FAX 602.956.9977

6 0 2 . 9 5 6 . 9 5 6 0

ORAL & FACIAL
SURGERY CENTER

2222 E. Highland Ave.
Suite #320
Phoenix, AZ 85016

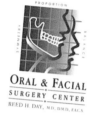

6200 S. McClintock Dr.
Suite #6A
Tempe, AZ 85283

ORAL & FACIAL
SURGERY CENTER
REED H. DAY, M.D., D.M.D., F.A.C.S.

2222 E. Highland Ave.
Suite #320
Phoenix, AZ 85016

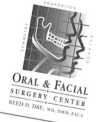

6200 S. McClintock Dr.
Suite #6A
Tempe, AZ 85283

ORAL & FACIAL
SURGERY CENTER
REED H. DAY, M.D., D.M.D., F.A.C.S.

Telephone:
602.956.9560
Fax 602.956.9977

6200 South McClintock Drive
Suite #6A
Tempe, AZ 85283

Client
Oral & Facial Surgery Center
Design Firm
Sullivan Marketing & Communication
Phoenix, Arizona
Designer
Jack Sullivan

ORAL & FACIAL
SURGERY CENTER

CCSSO · AACRAO · NCES

SPEEDEExPRESS

Council of Chief State School Officers
One Massachusetts Avenue, N.W.
Suite 700
Washington, D.C. 20001-1431

SPEEDEExPRESS

Council of Chief State School Officers, One Massachusetts Ave., N.W., Suite 700, Washington, D.C. 20001-1431

American Association of Collegiate Registrars and Admissions Officers, One Dupont Circle, N.W., Suite 370, Washington, D.C. 20036-1110

SPEEDEExPRESS

Client
Council of Chief State School Officers
Design Firm
Dever Designs
Laurel, Maryland
Designer
Jeffrey L. Dever

HOSPICE OF
HUMBOLDT

Client
Hospice of Humboldt
Design Firm
Jeff Fisher LogoMotives
Portland, Oregon
Designer
Jeff Fisher

Board of Directors

Linda Marcuz
President

Matt Dennis
Vice President

Susan McG...

2010 Myrtle Avenue
Eureka, CA 95501

Non-Profit Organization
U. S. Postage
P A I D
Permit No. 139
Eureka, CA 95501

2010 Myrtle Avenue
Eureka, CA 95501

707/445-8443
Fax: 707/445-2209

...ger

Laurie Watson-Stone

Margery Young

Executive Director

Paul Mueller

Medical Director

Kim Bauriedel, MD

2010 Myrtle Avenue • Eureka, CA 95501 • 707/445-8443 • Fax: 707/44...

HOSPICE OF HUMBOLDT

HOSPICE OF HUMBOLDT

2010 Myrtle Avenue
Eureka, CA 95501

Non-Profit Organization
U. S. Postage
P A I D
Permit No. 139
Eureka, CA 95501

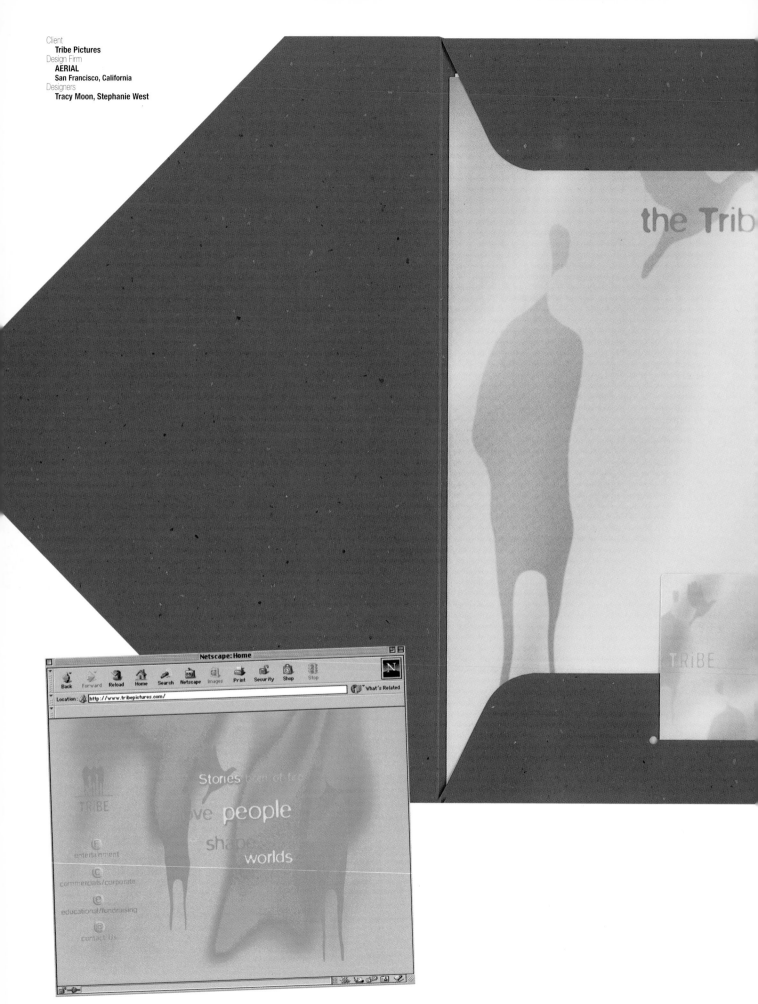

Client
Tribe Pictures
Design Firm
AERIAL
San Francisco, California
Designers
Tracy Moon, Stephanie West

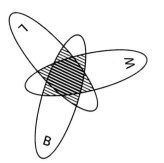

Client
Levin • Breidenbach • Wade
Design Firm
Levin • Breidenbach • Wade
Mill Valley, California
Designer
Jeff Breidenbach

LEVIN·BREIDENBACH·WADE

strategic communication + design

| L | B |
| W | • |

| 2 | 3 |
| B | D |

LEVIN·BREIDENBACH·WADE

LEVIN·BREIDENBACH

APPROVAL

TO:

PROJECT:

JOB NUMBER:

This
indic

LEVIN·BREIDENBACH·WADE

strategic communication + design

124 locust avenue - mill valley, ca 94941

T: 415 389 9813   F: 415 389 9815
124 locust avenue - mill valley, ca 94941   L-B-W.com

LEVIN·BREIDENBACH·WADE, LLC

LEVIN·BREIDENBACH·WADE, LLC

CHANGE ORDER

CLIENT: RIGHTTURNRETAIL

PROJECT: TRADE SHOW BOOTH

PER: SCOTT JORDAN

BY: JEFF BREIDENBACH

Description:

Make the following add

1. Design RightTurnR

2. Redesign 4 banner

3. RightTurnRetail

4. Design signage f

5. Size logos to b

6. Oversee prod

7. Supply abov

Estimated

strategic communication + design

F A X

TO:

COMPANY:

FAX #:

RE:

DATE:

FROM:

NO. PAGES:

LEVIN·BREIDENBACH·WADE

strategic communication + design

Lisa Levin

T: 415 389 9813   F: 415 389 9815   E: lisa@L-B-W.com
124 locust avenue · mill valley, ca 94941 L-B-W.com

903 minna street · san francisco, ca 94103   T: 415 581 1529   F: 415 581 1525   L-B

317

BOULLIOUN

BOULLIOUN

Client
  Boullioun Aviation Services
Design Firm
  Hornall Anderson Design Works, Inc.
  Seattle, Washington
Designers
  Jack Anderson, Katha Dalton,
  Belinda Bowling, Ryan Wilkerson

Stan's

WE DISPENSE SERVICE

ALBUQUERQUE
2101 Columbia Drive SE
Albuquerque, NM 87106

T: 505.247.3707
F: 505.247.4259

DENVER
4050 Globeville Rd.
Denver, CO 80216

T: 303.296.7533
F: 303.296.7559

EL PASO
11394 James Watt Dr.
Unit 308
El Paso, TX 79935

T: 915.598.4578
F: 915.598.4582

LUBBOCK
9002 Hwy 87
Lubbock, TX 79382

T: 806.748.1959
F: 806.748.0699

NORMAN
2776 Broce Dr.
Norman, OK 73072

T: 405.292.1857
F: 405.292.1857

BILLINGS
P.O. Box 80686
Billings, MT 59108-0686

www.WeDispenseService.com

Stan's

Client
Stan's
Design Firm
Rick Johnson & Company
Albuquerque, New Mexico
Designer
Tim McGrath

2101 Columbia Drive SE, Albuquerque, NM 87106

Stan's

Bob Lanaghan
Branch Manager

P.O. Box 80686
Billings, MT 59108-0686

V: 406.247.1987
M: 406.861.1857
E: BobL@WeDispenseService.com

Stan's
WE DISPENSE SERVICE

2101 Columbia Drive SE
Albuquerque, NM 87106

Stan's

WE DISPENSE SERVICE

Vitality   Ocean Spray   **Sunkist**

www.WeDispenseService.com

Maveron LLC
800 Fifth Avenue
Suite 4100
Seattle, WA
98104

www.maveron.com

maveron

Judy Z. Neuman
jneuman@maveron.com

(P) 206.447.1300
(F) 206.470.1150

Maveron LLC
800 Fifth Avenue
Suite 4100
Seattle, WA
98104

maveron

Maveron LLC
800 Fifth Avenue
Suite 4100
Seattle, WA
98104

www.maveron.com

(P) 206.447.1300
(F) 206.470.1150

maveron

maveron

Client
Maveron
Design Firm
**Hornall Anderson Design Works, Inc.
Seattle, Washington**
Designers
Jack Anderson, Margaret Long

Client
Trellis Fund
Design Firm
Greenfield/Belser Ltd.
Washington, D.C.
Designers
Burkey Belser, Chris Paul

1400 16th Street, NW
Suite 710
Washington, DC 20036

202.939.3399 telephone
202.939.3392 facsimile

1400 16th Street, NW
Suite 710
Washington, DC 20036

202.939.3399 telephone
202.939.3392 facsimile

Client
MGA
Design Firm
Kristin Odermatt Design
Santa Monica, California
Designers
Kristin Odermatt, Deanna McClure

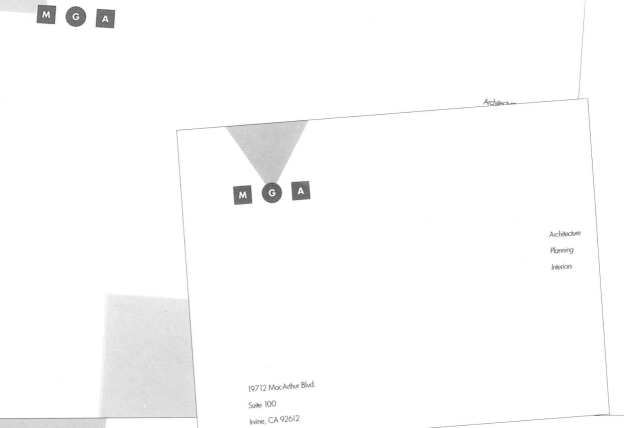

M G A

Architecture
Planning
Interiors

19712 MacArthur Blvd.
Suite 100
Irvine, CA 92612

M G A

Architecture
Planning
Interiors

MANNING PRODUCTIONS, INC.

Client
Manning Productions Inc.
Design Firm
JOED Design Inc.
Elmhurst, Illinois
Art Director
Edward Rebek
Designer
Adriana Mulligan

DOUGLAS MANNING
dmanning@manningproductions.com

MANNING PRODUCTIONS, INC.

224 North Des Plaines Street, Suite 250
Chicago, Illinois 60661
p 312.756.1100
f 312.756.1200

www.manningproductions.com

224 North Des Plaines Street | Suite 250 | Chicago, Illinois 60661

MANNING PRODUCTIONS, INC.

MANNING PRODUCTIONS, INC.

224 North Des Plaines Street, Suite 250
Chicago, Illinois 60661
p 312.756.1100
f 312.756.1200
www.manningproductions.com

MANNING PRODUCTIONS, INC. | www.manningproductions.com

f 312.756.1200 | p 312.756.1100 | Chicago, Illinois 60661 | Suite 250 | 224 North Des Plaines Street

MANNING PRODUCTIONS, INC.

224 North Des Plaines Street | Suite 250 | Chicago, Illinois 60661

CAPTIVATING, EDUCATING, MOTIVATING

Client
Miguel A. Ledezma Photographer
Design Firm
Kathleen Hatch Design
Dallas, Texas
Designer
Kathleen Hatch

MIGUEL ANGEL LEDEZMA

PHOTOGRAPHER

P.O. BOX 191721

DALLAS, TX 75219

214.793.5635 PH

FAX FORM

DATE:

TO:

FAX #:

FROM:

FAX #:

PAGES:

SUBJECT:

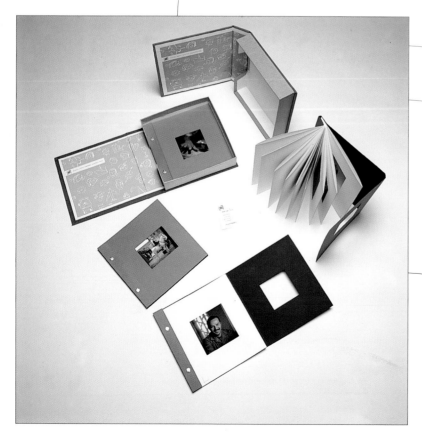

MIGUEL ANGEL LEDEZMA

PHOTOGRAPHER

P.O. BOX 191721

DALLAS, TX 75219

214.793.5635 PH

miguelaledezma@netscape.net

M

MIGUEL ANGEL LED

PHOTOGRAPHER

P.O. BOX 191721

DALLAS, TX 75219

214.793.5635 PH

MIGUEL ANGEL LEDEZMA

PHOTOGRAPHER

P.O. BOX 191721

DALLAS, TX 75219

miguelaledezma@netscape.net

M

MIGUEL ANGEL LEDEZMA

PHOTOGRAPHER

P.O. BOX 191721

DALLAS, TX 75219

214.793.5635 PH

conceptual capital

www.conceptualcapital.com

Conceptual Capital Ltd   mail@conceptualcapital.com

conceptual capital

ilya@conceptualcapital.com

conceptual capital

I thought you'd like to see this

ilya@conceptualcapital.com

Conceptual Capital Ltd

conceptual capital

conceptual capital

Conceptual Capital Ltd

Conceptual Capital Ltd
Ilya Nykin

314 989 9800 Telephone
314 989 9801 Facsimile

1155 Francis Place
St. Louis, MO 63117 USA

ilya@conceptualcapital.com

Client
  Conceptual Capital Ltd.
Design Firm
  Ed Mantels-Seeker
  St. Louis, Missouri
Designer
  Ed Mantels-Seeker

invisuals
Insightful imaging.

Client
Invisuals
Design Firm
Hess Design, Inc.
Natick, Massachusetts
Designer
Karyn Goba

invisuals
Insightful imaging.

Jeff Davidson

www.invisuals.com | email: jld@invisuals.com

| 281 SUMMER STREET | BOSTON MA | 02210 |
| TEL 617|542|5995 | FAX 617|482|1899 |

invisuals
Insightful imaging.

281 SUMMER STREET | BOSTON | MA | 02210

invisuals
Insightful imaging.

www.invisuals.com |

| 281 SUMMER STREET | BOSTON | MA | 02210 |
| TEL 617|542|5995 | FAX 617|482|1899 |

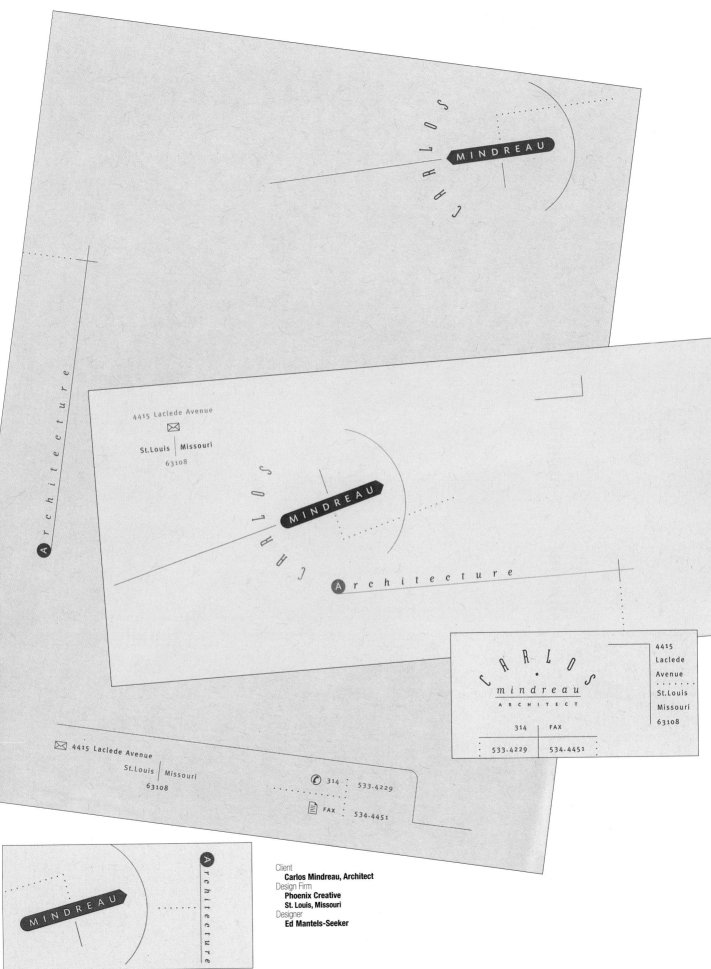

Client
Carlos Mindreau, Architect
Design Firm
Phoenix Creative
St. Louis, Missouri
Designer
Ed Mantels-Seeker

10 Blackstone Valley Place, Lincoln, RI 02865

Client
Autocrat, Inc.
Design Firm
Adkins/Balchunas
Providence, Rhode Island
Designers
Jerry Balchunas,
Michelle Phaneuf,
Susan DeAngelis

10 Blackstone Valley Place, Lincoln, RI 02865 401-333-3300 Fax: 401-333-3719

Client
Jane Brown Interiors
Design Firm
Julia Tam Design
Palos Verdes, California
Designer
Julia Tam

Jane Brown Interiors

Jane Brown Interiors

Jane Brown Interiors

Interiors

32 Hillcrest Meadows ❧ Rolling Hills Estates ❧ CA 90274

32 Hillcrest Meadows ❧ Rolling Hills Estates, CA 90274 ❧ 310.54

Jane Brown Interiors

Jane Brown, *Interior Designer*

32 Hillcrest Meadows
Rolling Hills Estates, CA 90274
Tᴇʟ 310.544.0625
Fᴀx 310.544.0635
E-Mᴀɪʟ: janewbrown@earthlink.net

Client
Alphabet Soup
Design Firm
Sayles Graphic Design
Des Moines, Iowa
Art Director, Designer, Illustrator
John Sayles

Client
connect.com
Design Firm
VWA Group
Dallas, Texas
Designer
Rhonda Camp Warren

Ted L. Snider, Jr.
President

connect.com

124 West Capitol Avenue
Suite 250
Little Rock, AR 72201
501.401.7601
Mobile: 214.763.0222
Fax: 501.401.7628
E-mail: dsnider@connect.com

connect.com

connect.com

124 West Capitol Ave.

Suite 250

Little Rock, AR 72201

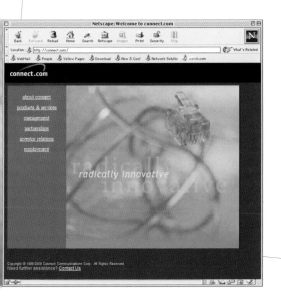

124 West Capitol Ave.

Suite 250

Little Rock, AR 72201

501.401.7700

Fax: 501.401.7799

Client
Clotia Wood and Metal Works
Design Firm
Insight Design Communications
Wichita, Kansas
Designers
Sherrie Holdeman, Tracy Holdeman

536 S. COMMERCE, WICHITA, KS 67202

536 S. COMMERCE
WICHITA, KS 67202

T 316-263-9722
F 316-263-1042

Client
**Clotia Wood and
Metal Works**
Design Firm
**Insight Design
Communications**
(continued)

"We believe in innovative design & unmistakable craftsmanshi

HARD SURFACES SPEAK HARD TRUTHS.

- We work with equal effectiveness from your drawing or o

- Our product is high-end in terms of its quality, decide middle-of-the-road in terms of its price.

- We produce hand-carvings and turnings and hand-for wrought-iron: all disguised as works of art.

- Everything we build is finished for its first appeal to the e for its eventual inability to be forgotten.

ONE MORE TRUTH.

We understand deadlines, budgets, and the unique needs of ev customer. At Clotia, we're business people with good ideas with very, very good hands.

CLOTIA
WOOD & METAL WORKS, INC.

CLOTIA
WOOD & METAL WORKS, INC.

BERT CLOTHIER

536 S. COMMERCE
WICHITA, KS 67202

T   316-263-9722
F   316-263-1042

Client
Clotia Wood and Metal Works
Design Firm
Insight Design Communications
(continued)

Custom or One-of-a kind Furniture

beds,
armoires, tables, chairs,
desks,
media centers...

Retail & Display Fixturing

specialty fixtures,
cashwraps,
custom tables,
innovative wall units...

Hospitality Furniture

case goods,
public area furniture,
reception/registration,
desks...

Custom Architectural Elements

entry doors, gates, fences,
light fixtures,
carved mantles,
fireplace screens...

Furniture Repair & Refinish

faux finishes,
antique restoration,
turnings & carvings,
finish repair...

Client
Boulder Business & Professional Women
Design Firm
Pollman Marketing Arts, Inc.
Boulder, Colorado
Designer
Jennifer Pollman

BOULDER BUSINESS AND PROFESSIONAL WOMEN
P.O. BOX 652
BOULDER, CO 80306

BOULDER BUSINESS AND
PROFESSIONAL WOMEN
P.O. BOX 652
BOULDER, CO 80306
303.415.3780
http:\\bcn.boulder.co.us\community\bpw

BOULDER BUSINESS AND PROFESSIONAL WOMEN   P.O. BOX 652   BOULDER, CO 80306   303.415.3780   http:\\bcn.boulder.co.us\community\bpw

PRINTING DONATED BY MASTERPRINT PRINTING

Client
  Continuum • 16 Market Square
Design Firm
  Ellen Bruss Design
  Denver, Colorado
Art Director
  Ellen Bruss
Designer
  Charles Carpenter
Calligrapher
  Greg Carr

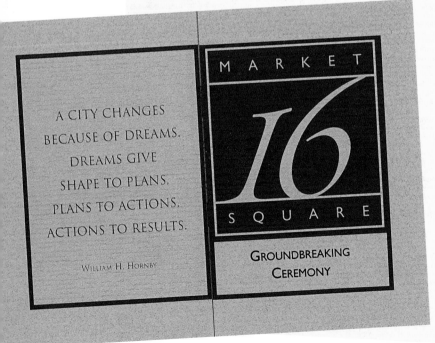

A CITY CHANGES
BECAUSE OF DREAMS.
DREAMS GIVE
SHAPE TO PLANS,
PLANS TO ACTIONS,
ACTIONS TO RESULTS.

WILLIAM H. HORNBY

GROUNDBREAKING
CEREMONY

Continuum Partners LLC
1610 15th Street
Denver, Colorado 80202

16 MARKET SQUARE

303.573.0050 voice
303.573.0011 fax

Client
Black River Center
Design Firm
JOED Design Inc.
Elmhurst, Illinois
Designer
Edward Rebek

BLACK
RIVER
CENTER

STARR
LITIGATION
SERVICES, INC

Client
Starr Litigation Services
Design Firm
Sayles Graphic Design
Des Moines, Iowa
Art Director, Designer, Illustrator
John Sayles

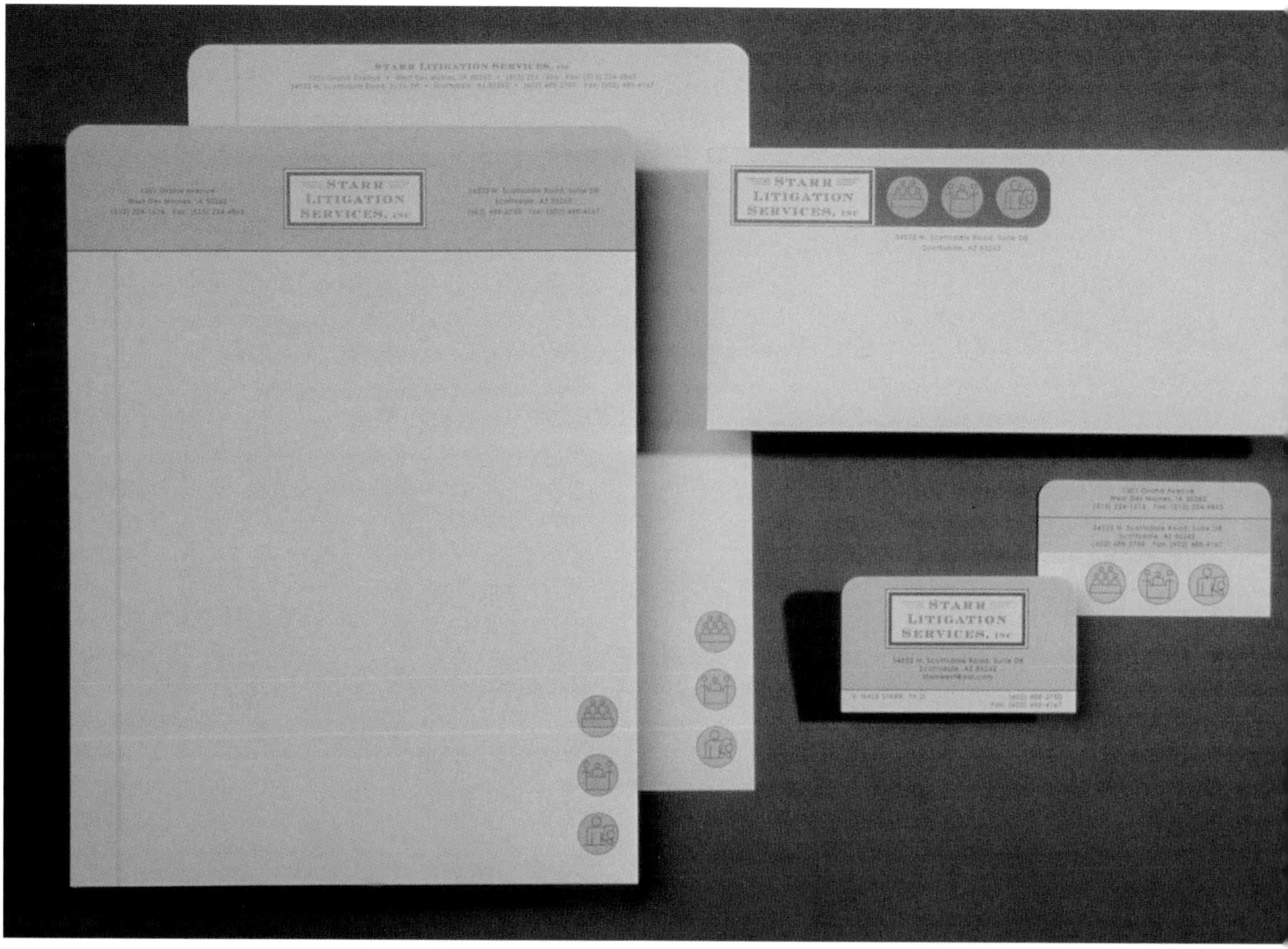

Client
Lanzen Investment Counsel
Design Firm
Dotzler Creative Arts
Omaha, Nebraska

LANZEN
INVESTMENT COUNSEL, INC
A Registered Investment Advisor

LANZEN
INVESTMENT COUNSEL, INC
A Registered Investment Advisor

LANZEN
INVESTMENT COUNSEL, INC
A Registered Investment Advisor
15037 Industrial Rd • Omaha, NE 68144-3233

LANZEN
INVESTMENT COUNSEL, INC
A Registered Investment Advisor

Gary W. Lanzen, CFP
President

15037 Industrial Rd • Omaha, NE 68144-3233
402-691-0422 ext. 203 • 800-424-2449
Fax 402-691-0420
E-mail: glanzen@radiks.net

Securities offered through Assist Investment Management Co., Inc.
7133 W 95th St. Suite 216 • Overland Park, KS 66212-2248 • 913-648-1881 • Member NASD, SIPC

15037 Industrial Rd • Omaha, NE 68144-3233 • 402-691-0422 • 800-424-2449 • Fax 402-691-0420

Securities offered through Assist Investment Management Co., Inc.
7133 W 95th St., Suite 216 • Overland Park, KS 66212-2248 • 913-648-1881 • Member NASD, SIPC

CASA DEL MAR

Client
Casa Del Mar
Design Firm
David Carter Design Assoc.
Dallas, Texas
Designer
Katherine Baronet

CASA DEL MAR

Warren Battle
Front Office Manager

1910 Ocean Front Walk
Santa Monica, CA 90405
Telephone 310.581.5533
Facsimile 310.581.5503

CASA DEL MAR

1910 Ocean Front Walk Santa Monica, California 90405

1910 Ocean Front Walk
Santa Monica, California 90405

CASA DEL MAR

CASA DEL MAR

CASA DEL MAR

1910 Ocean Front Walk
Santa Monica, California 90405
Telephone 310.581.5533
Facsimile 310.581.5503

Client
    echarge
Design Firm
    Hornall Anderson Design Works, Inc.
    Seattle, Washington
Designers
    Jack Anderson, Debra McCloskey,
    Kathy Saito, Holly Craven,
    Alan Copeland, Gretchen Cook,
    Henry Yiu

US: 500 UNION ST. SUITE 1000 SEATTLE, WA 98101

CANADA: 1770 W. 7TH AVE. SUITE 401 VANCOUVER, BC V6J 4Y6 | www.echarge.com

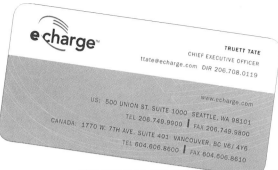

TRUETT TATE

CHIEF EXECUTIVE OFFICER

ttate@echarge.com DIR 206.708.0119

www.echarge.com

US: 500 UNION ST. SUITE 1000 SEATTLE, WA 98101
TEL 206.749.9900 | FAX 206.749.9800

CANADA: 1770 W. 7TH AVE. SUITE 401 VANCOUVER, BC V6J 4Y6
TEL 604.606.8600 | FAX 604.606.8610

eCharge Corporation

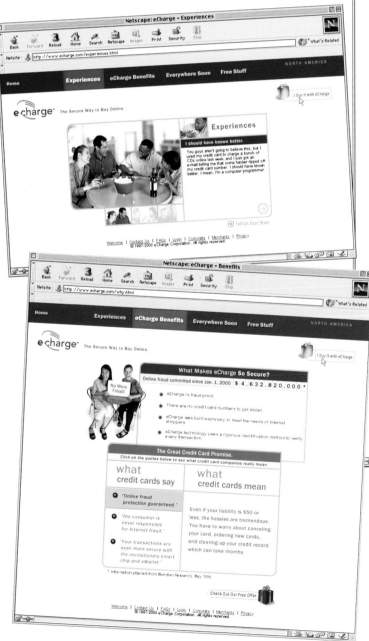

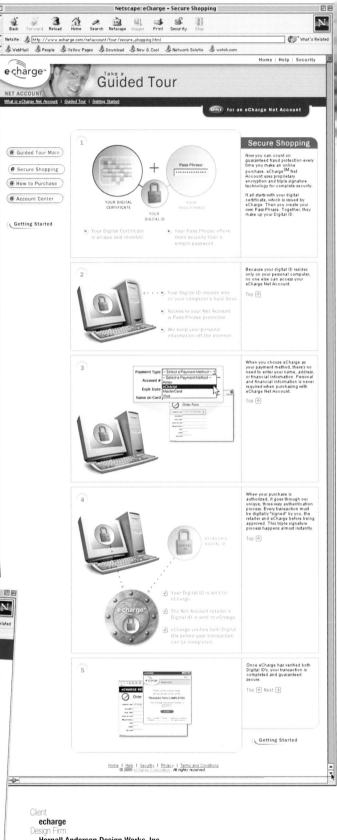

Client
   echarge
Design Firm
   Hornall Anderson Design Works, Inc.
(continued)

RON ERICKSON
CHAIRMAN
www.echarge.com

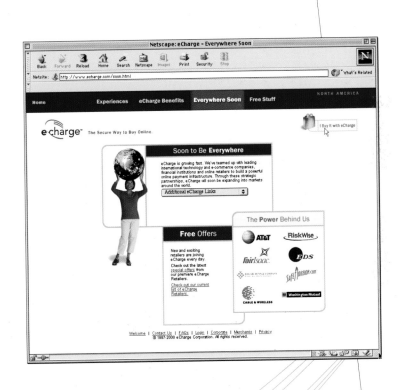

US: 500 UNION ST. SUITE 1000 SEATTLE, WA 98101 | TEL 206.749.9900 | FAX 206.749.9800

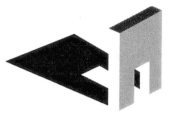

veenendaalcave

INTERIOR**DESIGN**

VeenendaalCave, Inc. 1275 Peachtree Street NE, Suite 400 Atlanta, Georgia 30309 **404.881.1811** fax 404.876.1

veenendaalcave

Leslie L. Hardy
ADMINISTRATIVE ASSISTANT

lhardy@vcave.com

1275 Peachtree St. NE, Suite 400
Atlanta, Georgia 30309
404.881.1811
fax 404.876.1289
vcave.com

fac~~simile~~

veenendaalcave

	Date
To	
	Fax #
Company	
	Project #
From	
	Page 1 of
CC	
Re	

☐ Urgent   ☐ For Review   ☐ As Requested   ☐ Please Reply

VeenendaalCave, Inc. 1275 Peachtree Street NE, Suite 400 Atlanta, Georgia 30309 **404.881.1811** fax 404.876.1289 vcave.com

letter of transmittal

veenendaalcave

	Date
To	
	Attention
Project	
Re	

We Are Sending You

☐ Via Courier
☐ Attached   ☐ Under Separate Cover
☐ By Hand   ☐ Via FedEX   ☐ Via U.S. Post

The Following Items

☐ Plans   ☐ Samples   ☐ Copy of Letter   ☐ Shop Drawings
☐ Prints   ☐ Specification   ☐ Change Order   ☐ Diskette(s)

☐ _____

Copies   **Date**   **Description**

veenendaal**cave**

...edy
...com

... NE, Suite 400
...0309

INTERIOR**DESIGN**

veenendaal**cave**

Tracy L. Glover
ASSOCIATE

tglover@vcave.com

1275 Peachtree St...
Atlanta, Georgia 3...
404.881.1811
fax 404.876.1289...
vcave.com

INTERIOR**DESIGN**

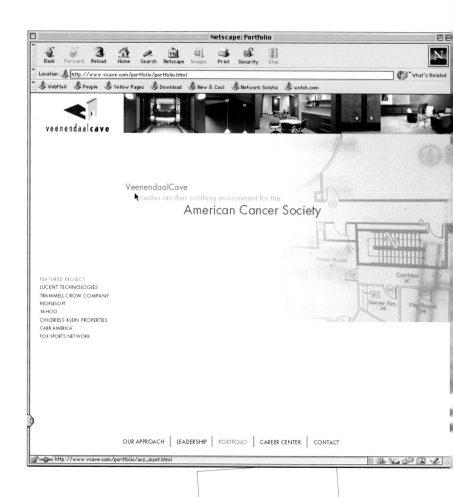

VeenendaalCave
creates another soothing environment for the
American Cancer Society

FEATURED PROJECT
LUCENT TECHNOLOGIES
TRAMMELL CROW COMPANY
PEOPLESOFT
YAHOO
CHILDRESS KLEIN PROPERTIES
CARR AMERICA
FOX SPORTS NETWORK

OUR APPROACH | LEADERSHIP | PORTFOLIO | CAREER CENTER | CONTACT

INTERIOR DESIGN · SPACE PLANNING

OUR APPROACH | LEADERSHIP | PORTFOLIO | CAREER CENTER | CONTACT

The Portal:
An architectural element that
represents transformation and
passage to a new environment.

Smith Cave & Assoc

VeenendaalCave

New exciting chan
Same exciting comp

Client
VeenendaalCave
Design Firm
Belyea
(continued)

VeenendaalCave, Inc.   1275 Peachtree Street NE, Suite 400   Atlanta, Georgia 30309

Client
Ivy Technologies
Design Firm
Eisenkramer Associates
St. Louis, Missouri
Designer
Ed Mantels-Seeker

The Ivy System:
The Practice
Information
Management
System
Designed
With Vision.

IVY *Technologies*

Dawn E. Holbrook
Customer Support

Ivy Technologies
4221 Forest Park Boulevard
St. Louis, Missouri 63108
314 652 5150

Manual

358

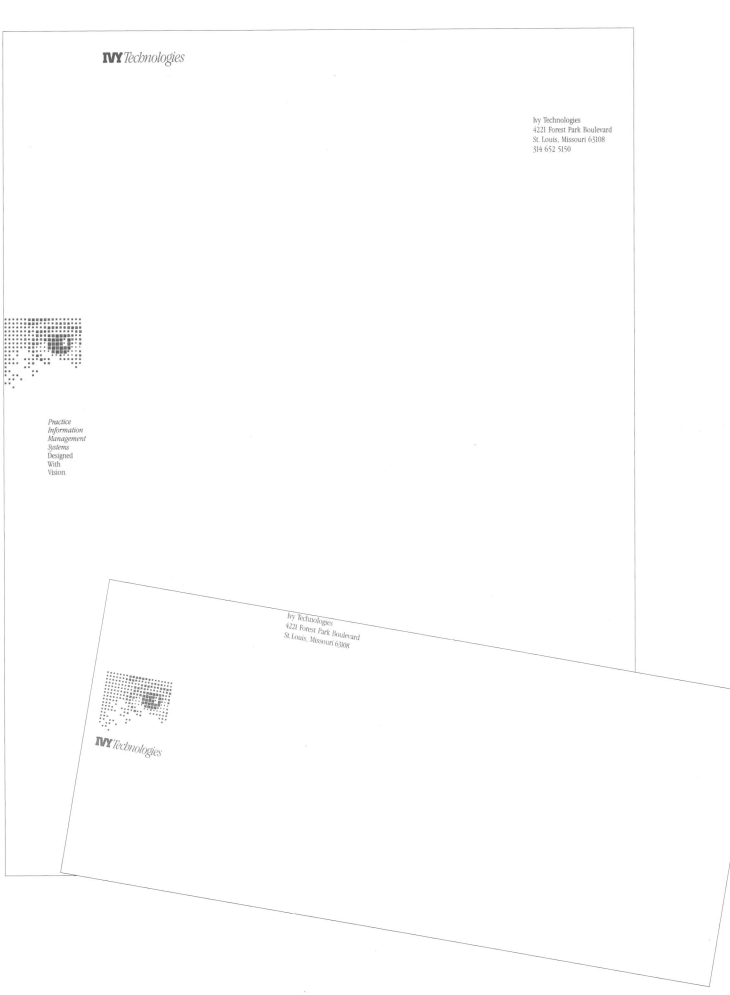

IVY Technologies

Ivy Technologies
4221 Forest Park Boulevard
St. Louis, Missouri 63108
314 652 5150

Practice
Information
Management
Systems
Designed
With
Vision.

Ivy Technologies
4221 Forest Park Boulevard
St. Louis, Missouri 63108

IVY Technologies

Client
Tileology
Design Firm
Dean Design/Marketing Group, Inc.
Lancaster, Pennsylvania
Designer
Jeff Phillips

245 Centerville Road • Lancaster, PA 17603

Stacy Smith

245 Centerville Road • Lancaster, PA
Phone: 717.290.7444 • Fax: 717.290.8
E-mail: mail@tileology.com • Internet: www.

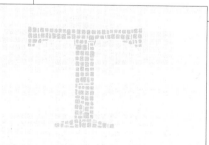

245 Centerville Road • Lancaster, PA 17603 • Phone: 717.290.7444 • Fax: 717.290.8075 • E-mail: mail@tileology.com • Internet: www.tileology.com

THE
ART
OF
FRENCH
LIVING™

MAISON DE FRANCE™

Moltissimo Building
10223 NE 10th Street
Bellevue, WA 98004
425-688-1078
ƒ 425-688-1130
maisondefrance.com

Client
  Maison de France
Design Firm
  Belyea
  Seattle, Washington
Art Director
  Patricia Belyea
Designer
  Christian Salas

MAISON DE FRANCE

From I-5 Take I-90 exit, travel across
bridge, take Bellevue Way exit,
follow Bellevue Way to vicinity
Or
Take 520 exit, travel across bridge,
take Bellevue Way exit to vicinity.

NE 10th Street
102nd Ave NE
103rd Ave NE
Access to 520
S
P
NE 8th Street   Access to I-405
BELLEVUE SQUARE
Bellevue Way NE

Mon · Sat   10am-7pm

MAISON DE FRANCE™

THE
ART
OF
FRENCH
LIVING™

Moltissimo Building
10223 NE 10th Street
Bellevue, WA 98004

MAISON DE FRANCE™

Moltissimo Building
10223 NE 10th Street
Bellevue, WA 98004
425-688-1078   ƒ 425-688-1130
maisondefrance.com

Client
StorageWay

Design Firm
Bruce Yelaska Design
San Francisco, California
Designer
Bruce Yelaska

2025 Gateway Place | Suite 116
San Jose, California 95110

2025 Gateway Place | Suite 116 | San Jose, California 95110
Tel: 408.467.8989 | Fax: 408.467.8998 | www.storageway.com

2025 Gateway Place | Suite 116
San Jose, California 95110

Peter Shambora
President & Chief Executive Officer

2025 Gateway Place | Suite 116 | San Jose, California 95110
Tel: 408.467.8991 | Fax: 408.467.8998
peters@storageway.com | www.storageway.com

Client
SleepTec
Design Firm
Insight Design Communications
Wichita, Kansas
Designers
Sherrie Holdeman, Tracy Holdeman

Client
SleepTec
Design Firm
Insight Design Communications
(continued)

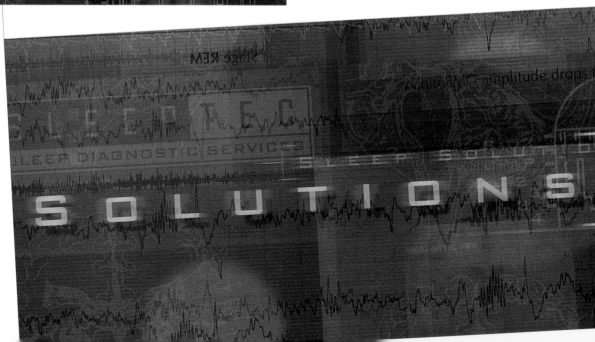

SLEEP TEC
SLEEP DIAGNOSTIC SERVICES

SLEEP SOLUTIONS

Stage REM

amplitude drops to lowest level

SLEEP SOLUTIONS

SLEEP TEC
SLEEP DIAGNOSTIC SERVICES

DUKE NAIPOHN/PRESIDENT

E-MAIL: TO7R@AOL.COM

2421 E. DOUGLAS, WICHITA, KS 67214
TEL: 316.683.2323 FAX: 316.683.1778

SLEEP SOLUTIONS

TREEHOUSE DESIGN

Client
Treehouse Design
Design Firm
Treehouse Design
Culver City, California
Designer
Tricia Rauen

TREEHOUSE DESIGN

10627 Youngworth Road
Culver City, CA 90230

TREEHOUSE DESIGN

10627 Youngworth Road
Culver City, CA 90230
310.204.2409 tel

TREEHOUSE DESIGN

10627 Youngworth Road, Culver City, CA 90230

310.204.2409 tel / 310.204.2517 fax

tr_treehouse@pacbell.net

Client
Tim Fuller
Design Firm
Boelts Bros. Associates
Tucson, Arizona
Designers
J. Boelts, K. Stratford,
E. Boelts, J. Stadnick

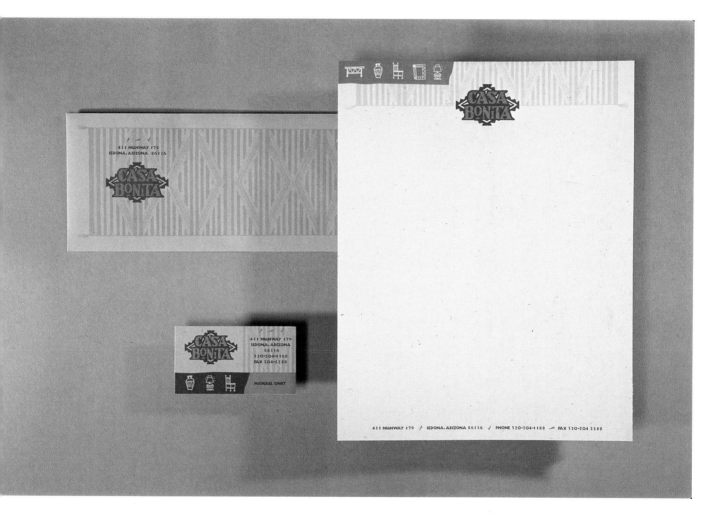

Client
Casa Bonita
Design Firm
Sayles Graphic Design
Des Moines, Iowa
Art Director, Designer, Illustrator
John Sayles

YOUR STRATEGIC
TECHNOLOGY PARTNER

Client
PC Assistance, Inc.
Design Firm
McElveney & Palozzi Design Group Inc.
Rochester, New York
Creative Director
William McElveney
Art Director, Designer
Lisa Williamson
Web Site Designers
PC Assistance, Inc.

ICRW

Client
International Center for Research on Women
Design Firm
Dever Designs
Laurel, Maryland
Designers
Jeffrey L. Dever, Emily Martin Kendall

ICRW

Charlotte Johnson-Welch
Public Health Specialist

**International Center for
Research on Women**
1717 Massachusetts Ave. N.W., Suite 302
Washington, DC 20036 USA
Phone: 202-797-0007, Fax: 202-797-0020
e-mail: icrw@igc.apc.org

ICRW

**International Center for
Research on Women**
1717 Massachusetts Ave. N.W., Suite 302
Washington, DC 20036 USA

International Center for Research on Women

With Our Compliments

onal Center for Research on Women
chusetts Avenue N.W., Suite 302, Washington, DC 20036 USA
02-797-0007, Fax: 202-797-0020, e-mail: icrw@igc.apc.org

ICRW

ICRW

International Center for Research on Women
1717 Massachusetts Ave. N.W., Suite 302 ▪ Washington, DC 20036 USA ▪ Te

International Center for Research on Women
1717 Massachusetts Avenue N.W., Suite 302, Washington, DC 20036 USA
Telephone: 202-797-0007, Fax: 202-797-0020, e-mail: icrw@igc.apc.org

Client
WatchGuard
Design Firm
Hornall Anderson
Design Works, Inc.
Seattle, Washington
Designers
Jack Anderson,
Lisa Cerveny, Kathy Saito,
Michael Brugman,
Holly Craven,
Belinda Bowling,
Tiffany Scheiblauer

316 Occidental Av
Seattle, WA 9810

WatchGuard **WatchGuard**

TECHNOLOGIES, INC.

316 Occidental Ave. S., Suite 200
Seattle, WA 98104

T 206.521.8340
F 206.521.8342
www.watchguard.com

WatchGuard®

TECHNOLOGIES, INC.

316 Occidental Ave. S., Suite 200
Seattle, WA 98104

WatchGuard®

TECHNOLOGIES, INC.

Client
WatchGuard
Design Firm
Hornall Anderson Design Works, Inc.
(continued)

WatchGuard®
TECHNOLOGIES, INC.

316 Occidental Ave. S., Suite 200
Seattle, WA 98104

T 206.521.8340
F 206.521.8342

www.watchguard.com

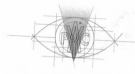

aypc rethink everything
Aumiller Youngquist, P.C.

architecture | interior design

p 847 253 3761
f 847 394 8320
www. aypc. com

III E. Busse Ave.
Suite 603
Mt.Prospect, IL
60056

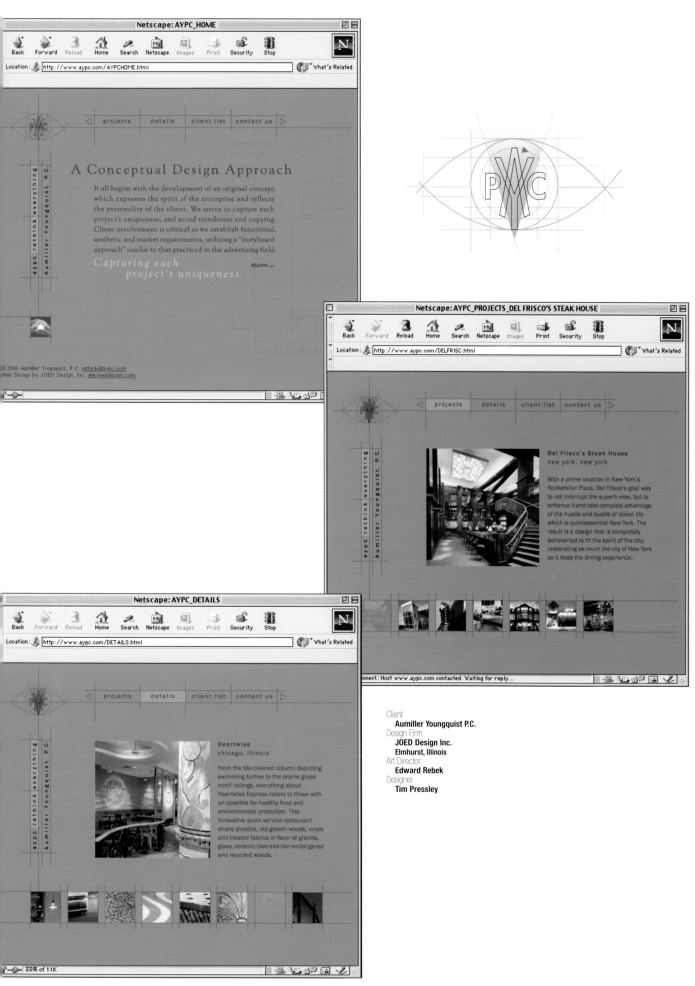

Netscape: AYPC_HOME

Location: http://www.aypc.com/AYPCHOME.html

projects   details   client list   contact us

aypc rethink everything   Aumiller Youngquist, P.C.

A Conceptual Design Approach

It all begins with the development of an original concept which expresses the spirit of the enterprise and reflects the personality of the client. We strive to capture each project's uniqueness, and avoid trendiness and copying. Client involvement is critical as we establish functional, aesthetic and market requirements, utilizing a "storyboard approach" similar to that practiced in the advertising field.

Capturing each project's uniqueness   more...

© 2000 Aumiller Youngquist, P.C. rethink@aypc.com
Web Design by JOED Design, Inc. www.joeddesign.com

Netscape: AYPC_PROJECTS_DEL FRISCO'S STEAK HOUSE

Location: http://www.aypc.com/DELFRISC.html

projects   details   client list   contact us

aypc rethink everything   Aumiller Youngquist, P.C.

Del Frisco's Steak House
new york, new york

With a prime location in New York's Rockefeller Plaza, Del Frisco's goal was to not interrupt the superb view, but to enhance it and take complete advantage of the hustle and bustle of street life - which is quintessential New York. The result is a design that is completely extroverted to fit the spirit of the city, celebrating as much the city of New York as it does the dining experience.

Connect: Host www.aypc.com contacted. Waiting for reply...

Netscape: AYPC_DETAILS

Location: http://www.aypc.com/DETAILS.html

projects   details   client list   contact us

aypc rethink everything   Aumiller Youngquist, P.C.

Heartwise
chicago, illinois

From the tile-covered column depicting swimming turtles to the prairie grass motif railings, everything about Heartwise Express caters to those with an appetite for healthy food and environmental protection. This innovative quick service restaurant shuns plastics, old growth woods, vinyls and treated fabrics in favor of granite, glass, ceramic tiles and non-endangered and recycled woods.

33% of 11K

Client
Aumiller Youngquist P.C.
Design Firm
JOED Design Inc.
Elmhurst, Illinois
Art Director
Edward Rebek
Designer
Tim Pressley

Client
internet eddie company
Design Firm
Design Room
Cleveland, Ohio
Designers
Chad Gordon, Kevi Rathge

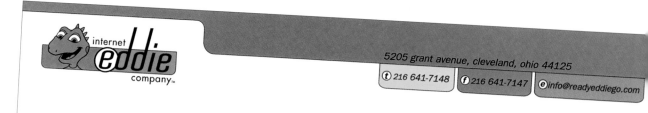

5205 grant avenue, cleveland, ohio 44125

(t) 216 641-7148   (f) 216 641-7147   (e)info@readyeddiego.com

5205 grant avenue, cleveland, ohio 44125

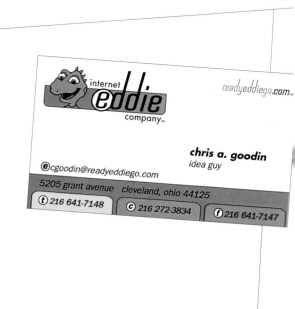

chris a. goodin
idea guy

(e)cgoodin@readyeddiego.com

5205 grant avenue   cleveland, ohio 44125

(t) 216 641-7148   (c) 216 272-3834   (f) 216 641-7147

readyeddiego.com

INDEX

DESIGN FIRMS
Symbols
30sixty design inc. 11

A
Adkins/Balchunas 48, 334
AERIAL 32, 58, 59, 140, 141, 142, 143, 254, 255, 262, 263, 314, 315
Artworks Advertising 42, 43, 138, 139
Axis Communications 224, 225, 226, 227

B
Belyea 30, 31, 129, 354, 355, 356, 357, 361
Bloch + Coulter Design Group 308, 309
Bjornson Design Associates, Inc. 128, 207, 238, 239, 273
Boelts Bros. Associates 108, 109, 370
Donato design 49
Bruce Yelaska Design 362, 363

C
Courage Design 72, 73, 222

D
David Carter Design Assoc. 28, 29, 200, 201, 283, 284, 285, 348, 349
Dean Design/Marketing Group, Inc 360
Design Room 382
Dever Designs 145, 186, 187, 203, 246, 248, 249, 250, 251, 311, 374, 375
Dotzler Creative Arts 96, 347

E
Ed Mantels-Seeker 330, 331
Eisenkramer Associates 358, 359
Ellen Bruss Design 218, 219, 344
Ervin Marketing Creative Comm. 120, 121

F
Fleishman-Hillard Design, St. Louis 16, 17, 22, 69, 117
Fly Graphics 98

G
Girvin, Inc. 8, 9, 36, 37, 188, 189, 214, 215, 216, 217
Gold & Associates 66, 78, 79, 126, 127
Goldforest 75, 244, 245
Greenfield/Belser Ltd. 18, 19, 91, 130, 131, 164, 165, 323
Grey Matter Design 170, 171

H
Halleck 82, 83, 179
Heart Graphic Design 266
Hess Design, Inc. 62, 286, 287, 332
Hornall Anderson Design Works, Inc. 13, 41, 44, 45, 60, 61, 64, 97, 102, 103, 114, 115, 148, 149, 150, 151, 152, 153, 168, 169, 172, 182, 183, 232, 233, 253, 260, 264, 265, 274, 275, 288, 289, 304, 305, 318, 319, 322, 350, 351, 352, 353, 376, 377, 378, 379
Hunt Weber Clark Assoc., Inc. 46, 99, 133

I
Insight Design Communications 338, 339, 340, 341, 342, 364, 365, 366, 367

J
Jeff Fisher LogoMotives 111, 122, 156, 157, 160, 208, 209, 228, 229, 230, 231, 240, 241, 242, 243, 261, 300, 301, 302, 303, 312, 313
Jensen Design Associates, Inc. 14, 15
JOED Design Inc. 74, 185, 326, 327, 345, 380, 381
Julia Tam Design 335

K
Kathleen Hatch Design 328, 329
Kiku Obata and Company 47, 106, 107
Kristin Odermatt Design 6, 7, 180, 181, 324, 325

L
Levin • Breidenbach • Wade 316, 317
Lorenz 174, 175
Love Packaging Group 100, 101, 176, 177

M
Maddock Douglas, Inc. 90
McDill Design 4, 5, 88, 89, 134, 135, 221
McElveney & Palozzi Design Group 25, 53, 63, 84, 85, 88, 124, 125, 306, 307, 372, 373

O
One of One/Imagearts 173

P
Phoenix Creative 10, 24, 39, 65, 105, 112, 113, 178, 299, 333
Pollman Marketing Arts, Inc. 21, 68, 123, 161, 167, 184, 343

R
Randi Wolf Design 20, 92, 93
Resco Print Graphics 80
Rick Johnson & Company 256, 257, 258, 259, 281, 320, 321
Rutgers University Publications 268, 269, 270, 271, 274, 276, 277, 278, 279

S
Sayles Graphic Design 23, 27, 38, 40, 52, 67, 81, 104, 110, 116, 132, 136, 144, 155, 166, 202, 223, 236, 247, 252, 267, 272, 280, 298, 336, 346, 371
Shimokochi/Reeves 137, 158, 159, 199, 206, 220
Studio Izbickas 198
Sullivan Marketing & Communications 146, 147, 194, 195, 282, 310

T
The Traver Company now Methodologie, Inc. 154, 190, 191, 237
Tom Fowler, Inc. 234, 235
Treehouse Design/Evenson Design 12, 204, 205, 368, 369
Tusk Studios 54, 55, 86, 87, 294, 295, 296, 297

U
über, inc. 192, 193

V
Visual Marketing Associates 33, 196, 197
VWA Group 34, 35, 50, 51, 56, 57, 70, 71, 76, 77, 94, 95, 118, 119, 337

W
Whitney Stinger, Inc. 26, 162, 163
William Homan Design 210, 211, 212, 213, 290, 291, 292, 293

CLIENTS
Symbols
1997 Iowa State Fair "Go For It" 252
1998 Iowa State Fair "Way Too Much Fun!" 280
1999 Iowa State Fair 38
2000 Iowa State Fair "Zero In" 67
30sixty design 11
801 Steak and Chop House 81

A
Abacus 28, 29
AERIAL 140, 141, 142, 143
Allied Capital 91
Alphabet Soup 336
American Marketing Association 166
AMP/Anne-Marie Petrie 160
Argent Hotel/San Francisco, The 16, 17
Artisan Partners 134, 135
Artworks Advertising 42, 43
Atwater Foods, Inc. 84, 85
Aumiller Youngquist P.C. 380, 381
Autocrat, Inc. 334
Avenue A 102, 103

B
Baker Group, The 62
Barrick Roofing 104
Beach House 32
Beverly Sassoon International 220
bHive 128
Big Daddy Photography 132
Big Island Candies 97
Black River Center 345
Bloch + Coulter Design Group 308, 309
Blue Nile 152, 153
Boston Unique Events 198
Boulder Business & Professional Women 343
Boullioun Aviation Services 318, 319
Brownstone Residential 282
Buena Vista College 155

C
Cantilever Technologies 90
Care Future 288, 289
Carlos Mindreau, Architect 333
Carnegie Endowment for International Peace 248, 249, 250, 251
Cary Pillo Lassen 30, 31
Casa Bonita 371
Casa Del Mar 348, 349
Casa Monica Hotel 78, 79
Centegy 179
Centex Multi-Family Co. 34, 35
City, The 290, 291, 292, 293
Clayton (MO) Chamber of Commerce 120, 121
CLEO's 54, 55
Clotia Wood and Metal Works 338, 339, 340, 341, 342
Conceptual Capital Ltd. 330, 331
connect.com 337
Consolidated Correctional Food Services 236
Continuum • 16 Market Square 344
CoolFish Grille and Wine Bar 48
Copper Sky Grill 41
Council of Chief State School Officers 311
craftopia.com 49
Cutler Travel Marketing 40
Cynd Snowboard Apparel 33
Cypress Center, The 204, 205

D

Dennis Crews 203
Dever Designs 186, 187
Distilled Images 58, 59

E

echarge 350, 351, 352, 353
Elliott Hotel, The (R.C. Hedreen) 190, 191
Employment Link 167
epods 172
epropose 99
ESM Consulting Engineers 237
etrieve 253
Eventra 234, 235
Executive Strategies 52
Exstream 88, 89

F

Fallbrook Engineering 174, 175
Ferguson, Wellman, Rudd, Purdy & Van Winkle, Inc 156, 157
Finishing Touch, The 298
Fly Graphics 98
Fox Theatre Tucson 108, 109
Future of Diabetics, Inc. 196, 197

G

Gabriel Consortium, Inc., The 145
GDC Enviro-Solutions, Inc. 210, 211, 212, 213
GeoTrust 129
Gettuit.com 274, 275
Gifted Gardener, The 178
Glen Ellen Carneros Winery 82, 83
Gold & Associates 66
Good Times Jazz Festival 202
Goodwin Tucker Group 223
Governor Hotel 300, 301, 302, 303
Grand Central Post 299
Grapefinds 260

H

Hardware.com 60, 61
Heavenly Stone 182, 183
Hess Design, Inc. 286, 287
Hospice of Humboldt 312, 313
Hotel Fort Des Moines 144
Hudson Community Fund, The 80
Hungry Camper 267

I

Image Tek 247
Imageware 4, 5
Imind Corporation 168, 169
Impli 44, 45
Improvisational Learning Systems 221
Intelligent Biocides 65
Intermountain/RKH 161
International Center for Research on Women 374, 375
internet eddie company 382

Invisuals 332
Ionis International 184
Iowa State Fair Blue Ribbon Foundation 116
Ivy Technologies 358, 359
izyx 12

J

Jacksonville Jazz Festival • WJCT 126, 127
Jane Brown Interiors 335
Jefferson Properties 118, 119
Jensen Design Associates, Inc. 14, 15
Joie de Vivre Hospitality 46
JPI 70, 71, 76, 77

K

Kay Johnson's Sing Out Productions 122
Kestrel Partners/Portico 218, 219
Kimpton Hotel + Restaurant Group 133
KVO Public Relations 170, 171

L

La Parisienne 273
Lanzen Investment Counsel 347
Las Vegas Odyssey 294, 295, 296, 297
LeRoy Village Green 306, 307
Levin • Breidenbach • Wade 316, 317
Lightmakers 222
Littlefield Unlimited Specialty Marketing 162, 163
Lodge at Woodcliff, The 53
LOGIS Ltd. 74
Love Packaging Group 100, 101

M

Maison de France 361
Manning Productions Inc. 326, 327
Mansion at MGM Grand, The 200, 201
Mary Brandon 199
Masterprint 123
Maveron 322
Mayer Bros. 124, 125
Merchandising East 224, 225, 226, 227
MGA 324, 325
Miguel A. Ledezma Photographer 328, 329
Mitchell and Hugeback Architects 24
Monsanto Company/Nidus Center 112, 113
Mr. Reynold's Limousine Service 272
MYRIO 216, 217

N

New York Urban League 117

O

Old Market Street 92, 93
Olson Sundberg Kundig Allen 188, 189
Omnigraphics 246
Onyx Software 304, 305
Oral & Facial Surgery Center 310
Oxbow 256, 257, 258, 259

P

Paris Casino Resort 283
Pattee Enterprises "Arts & Crafts Conference" 110
Patton Boggs LLP 164, 165
PC Assistance, Inc. 372, 373
Peggy Sundays 261
Pepper Hamilton LLP 18, 19
Phoenix Property Co. 50, 51, 56, 57
PhotoZone 13
Pinnacle Education 194, 195
PlanetExchange 207
planetpackaging.com 75
Princess Peahead.com 173
Psomas 180, 181

R

Randi Wolf Design 20
Rats 238, 239
Recharge 114, 115
Rhea Anna Photography 72, 73
Rick Johnson & Company 281
RJ Muna 254, 255
Rocky Mountain Anglers 68
ROR 206
Rosewood Hotels 94, 95
RUNet 2000 274, 276, 277, 278, 279
Rutherford Investment Management 228, 229, 230, 231

S

Saint Theresa's at South Gate 47
San Francisco Giants/Pacific Bell 22
Sayles Graphic Design 27
Sbemco International 136
Seaboard Building 148, 149, 150, 151
Seattle Public Library 8, 9
Seattle Seahawks 240, 241, 242, 243
Shaw Center, The 146, 147
Shimokochi/Reeves 137
Shoplocal.com 214, 215
Simply Cruises 39
Skinner Law 266
SleepTec 364, 365, 366, 367
Smuckers Quality Beverages 158, 159
Space Needle 264, 265
St. Louis Sports Commission 10
Stan's 320, 321
Starr Litigation Services 346
Starry Night 185
StorageWay 362, 363

Stray Dog Cafe 154
Streamworks 64
Surfacine Consumer Products 105
Sutherland Asbill & Brennan LLP 130, 131

T

TEAAM Sports Agency 244, 245
Technology Advancement Group 21
The Argent Hotel/San Francisco 16, 17
The Baker Group 62
The City 290, 291, 292, 293
The Cypress Center 204, 205
The Elliott Hotel (R.C. Hedreen) 190, 191
The Finishing Touch 298
The Gabriel Consortium, Inc. 145
The Gifted Gardener 178
The Hudson Community Fund 80
The Lodge at Woodcliff 53
The Mansion at MGM Grand 200, 201
The Shaw Center 146, 147
The Vein Center 106, 107
The Washington Monarch Hotel 69
Therapon 176, 177
Tileology 360
Tim Fuller 370
Timbuktuu Coffee Bar 23
Treehouse Design 368, 369
Trellis Fund 323
TriAd 208, 209
Tribe Pictures 314, 315
Trinity Life in Jesus 96
Trinity Project 111
Tusk Studios 86, 87

U

über, inc. 192, 193
University Inn & Conference Center 268, 269, 270, 271

V

VeenendaalCave 354, 355, 356, 357
Vein Center, The 106, 107
Veneklasen Associates 6, 7
violet.com 262, 263
Virtuoso 284, 285
Vista.com 36, 37

W

Washington Monarch Hotel, The 69
WatchGuard 376, 377, 378, 379
Watt Farms Country Market 63
Whitney Stinger, Inc. 26
Witlyn Homes 138, 139

X

Xelus 25
XOW! 232, 233